The Way of the

Jane Ball and Ch:

DEDICATION

This book is dedicated to our darling grandchildren, Léa, Emma and Arlen. May they find some inspiration from the exploits of their grandmothers.

CONTENTS

PLACE INDEX

ACKNOWLEDGMENTS

We would like to thank all our family and friends who supported us before and during our pilgrimage along the Camino Way. In particular we would like to thank Matthew for helping us set up our blog, all the people who gave us lovely and extremely useful walking-related gifts, all those who sent us good luck cards and messages before we began and well done messages when we returned, all those who e-mailed us, texted us and who commented on the blog. However, there is one thank you that must rank above all others and that is to Henry, without whose practical and psychological support our journey would have been very much more difficult. We would like to thank John Brierley for producing his incredibly useful guidebook. Finally we would like to say thank you to all the lovely pilgrims we met on the Way who enriched our journey, amongst whom were: Ingo, Cecelia, Susie, Bill, Leo, Darren, Bethany, Jenny, Brian, Diego, Francoise, Claude, Hubert, Ayn, Michael, Sandra, John, Kate, Terrence, Jacob, Ella, Carole, Rafael and Meg.

CHAPTER ONE INTRODUCTION

First of all who are we? We are two sisters, Jane and Charlotte, and are the middle two of a family of four siblings *(Jane, the elder – on left, Charlotte, the younger, on right)*, raised in Kent with their brothers, Mark and Hugh. The family was unorthodox and Roman Catholic. All four siblings lapsed from Catholicism in adulthood despite convent and Catholic education from the age of four. As children we tended to split into Mark and Jane as the eldest and Charlotte and Hugh as the youngest, with the older pair feeling responsible for the younger ones and the younger ones feeling picked on by the older siblings – t'was probably ever thus in most large families, but perhaps more so in this one as our parents did not practice some of the traditional parenting skills and the kids had to compensate. We all went on to have our own families and careers, living around the UK and in America. As adults we found we had maintained a real family bond, possibly forged by some of the adversities faced when we were young. With respect to the photo above, Charlotte always maintained that the gold coloured piping band that went around the top of our strange school hats was intended to represent a halo; this might explain her penchant for surrounding herself with a luminous glow in in future photos.

In part because our children were of an age (Jane's and Charlotte's), we two sisters had gone on holiday together for a number of years and these holidays morphed over time from bucket-and-spade seaside camping hols to cottage breaks, to more serious walking breaks without the (now adult) kids. Walking had, invidiously and surreptitiously, become an important part of our holiday relaxation. Separately, Jane and her husband, Henry, had become modest long-distance walkers upon their retirements. Gradually the Pennine Way, the Coast-to-Coast from St Bees to Robin Hood's Bay and the West Highland Way were all traversed. The South Downs Way was completed in stages as they lived on the doorstep. Charlotte then joined in for The Cumbrian Way and the Lakeland Haute Route. In addition, every Easter the extended family would gather in the Lake District and some walking would take place. Whilst not being hugely outdoorsy people, we had enormously enjoyed many camping holidays together when the children were young.

A picture might be forming now of two very outward-bound oriented women. This would not be an entirely accurate picture. Yes, we knew our way around a pair of walking boots and some wet-weather over-trousers, but apart from the occasional amble on the Ashdown Forest (Jane) or sorties with partners and friends into the Peak District (Charlotte) we did very little in between the big annual "one offs". We were notorious in the family for being at the back of the pack on group walks and Henry swore blind that he spent twice as much time standing still waiting for us to catch up as he did walking. Our physiques were a long way from the lean fell runner's or the sturdy athlete's and both of us nursed on-going health issues. So why were we thinking about a five-hundred mile walk in a country whose language neither of us spoke and where we would be carrying all our kit for the entire walk? In addition, neither of us were great travellers. Trips abroad in the past to such places as Italy and France to see relatives or take holidays and trips to the USA to visit our brother had largely been "project planned" by Henry, who enjoyed doing that sort of thing. On the Camino trip we would have to be far more self-reliant. We had both worked as professional women, one in the education sector, and the other in the health sector and were used to making decisions and directing affairs. But wandering around a bit in Spain for five or so weeks was going to take us right out of our comfort zones.

Where were we going? Many readers will know that the Camino Way is not just one specific pilgrimage route, but in fact many, determined by where one starts the walk (central France, Southern Spain, Portugal, Northern Spain, one's very own doorstep, etc.) but all culminating in Santiago de Compostela in North West Spain. As with the pilgrims of yore, one could walk or ride. In the modern day, cycling is also a travel option. Today to claim official recognition of achieving the pilgrimage, walkers have to complete the final 100 kilometres, horse riders the final 100 kilometres and cyclists the final 200 kilometres. No doubt in the past many pilgrims who could afford it took rides in wagons, on horses and donkeys and trips on boats to reduce the difficulty of travelling by foot, to speed up the time it would take and to reduce the danger somewhat. In the modern day the difficulty, danger and length of time required is so reduced that the "rules" about the final 100 or 200 kilometres have been applied. We were going to be walking the Camino Frances, the route from St Jean Pied de Port, a French village in the foothills of the Pyrenees, through Pamplona, Logroño, Burgos, Leon and Ponferrada to Santiago de Compostela – a journey of approximately 800 kilometres or 500 miles.

We had been talking for ages about walking the Camino Way in the spring of 2013, after Charlotte retired on 20 January 2013 when she was sixty. Whilst doing the Coast-to-Coast long-distance walk with Henry in 2009, Jane had met a young Methodist Minister, Helen, who had completed the Camino Frances the previous year. Helen's account of her walk stirred in Jane a real desire to do the walk; it sounded like such a personally fulfilling thing to do. Henry, however, was determined instead to complete all 214 Wainwright fells in the Lake District over the following few years so his priorities were different. Jane would need to find another walking companion and fortunately Charlotte was up for it, but not until she had retired and only when her ancient cat, Gilbert, had ascended to the great catnip pasture in the sky. In time both these conditions were fulfilled so we sisters would now have to deliver on our ambition.

And why are we writing about it when there are so many Camino guide books and individual accounts from pilgrims on the bookshelves already? To many it might seem that the whole world has caught a verbal diarrhoea bug, filling the electronic media with mindless personal inanities, believing that one's own world is of the remotest interest to other people, that there is something to say and that anyone can say it in an interesting way. Now we appear to be falling into this same trap of self-delusion. Well, this book is largely for our families and us. Having said that, before we set out we both enjoyed reading all sorts of accounts of other people's Camino Way pilgrimages. This was notwithstanding the fact that some were not particularly well-written. We were greedy to begin the adventure, but could only do so vicariously. If this book acts to sate anybody else's pre-Camino appetite, all well and good. It is not an account of how to prepare oneself for the pilgrimage – how to train, what to pack, what to take- what to leave, what to visit en route. Nor shall we advise on the best hostels, the optimum distance to travel each day or how to make friends as one travels. We have no wish to suggest others should "do" the Camino in a certain way – fast, slow, in stages, with or without baggage support, in company or solo. What worked or failed for us might be entirely different for another person. But it is an account of how it impacted on us – both at the time, but, almost more importantly, much later, long after we had returned. We are two people, as ordinary as the next person – which is to say, unique. So our story is peculiar to us, but the reader might find the book of passing interest and if not, then it is no problem – our grandchildren will perhaps, in due course, realise what they can achieve if they challenge themselves and rise to that challenge. What we have found is that we cannot let our Camino pilgrimage go, despite its being nearly a year since we set off. We sensed that writing a book might be cathartic, confirmatory and clarifying.

So, very briefly, that is us, two retired English women, setting out on a huge adventure.

CHAPTER TWO   THINKING ABOUT IT

We had done some planning (bought the guide book), but little serious thinking and had yet to be sufficiently committed as to book the plane tickets. However, come 1 January 2013 we were determined to begin our training and planning proper. We even started a blog as part of the psychological preparation as Jane's son, Matthew, dragged his Mum into the electronic 21st century getting us ready to keep any interested friends and family in touch with where we were and how we were coping with the walk. We had started telling friends and family, in part because we were excited, but also to make the idea of walking the Camino Frances real and to stop us retracting and backing out altogether.

As an aside, we had neither of us, up to the start of the Camino adventure, jumped on board the social media bandwagon. We had not joined Facebook or Twitter and had never had cause to write blogs before. We were, however, concerned to be leaving family for a reasonably long period of time with only the occasional phone call and text to maintain links. We were persuaded that writing a blog would mean as many people within the extended family who wanted to could keep track of our wellbeing, as could any friends who might be interested. We did not really believe we would be able to keep it up as we would be completely dependent on whatever technology we bumped into along the route. In the following pages we have included some of our blog entries to demonstrate how we did overcome what, for us, was a considerable technological challenge.

Blog (Jane) on 1st January 2013

Well, I've started! 9.7 miles on the Ashdown Forest and 2,000ft of elevation -- very muddy and slippy but beautiful clear blue skies. I was totally kn......d and I wasn't even carrying the pack -- Henry was. I am seriously considering exploring the pros and cons of hiring an Himalayan Sherpa!!!!

The intention is to do two of these walks a week --- we'll see.

For all of December, January, February and March Charlotte suffered from seemingly endless rounds of chest infections and bronchitis, necessitating numerous doses of varied antibiotics. (It was not until after our return from Spain that she discovered that childhood double pneumonia had left her with a permanent lung problem – when we set off on May 1st we thought she just had to shift a bit of a residual cough!) She was, inevitably, rather down and also thought the Camino dream was slipping away as no training walks were undertaken and the chest got worse rather than better. Charlotte dragged herself into the hospital trust where she worked on the day of her retirement send off, but told the family she was postponing a 60th birthday party to the Summer. Well, little did she know! With much careful engineering the extended family secretly descended on brother Mark's house in Birmingham, whilst Charlotte's son, Nat, having invited his mum down on the pretext of an early birthday party for her grandson, then told his Mum he thought it would be nice to pop up to Mark's to say "Hi". Nat drove her and his family oh so very, very slowly up from Oxford to ensure they were the last to arrive. Surprise!!! Charlotte began to feel human again and blow the chest! Almost all the gifts Charlotte received were Camino-related and psychologically, walking the Camino Way was once more a very real prospect.

A representation of the Camino Way in cake, from the Pyrenees to the cathedral at Santiago with a huge central walking boot for Charlotte's 60th birthday.

Part of Charlotte's preparation was to think how she would manage the emotional impact of walking a Catholic pilgrimage route having seriously lapsed from the faith. As a lesbian feminist woman she was being asked by friends why she was doing this and how she would cope with the interface of her childhood beliefs and her adult way of life. After much reflection and after recognising the import and symbolism of some of the Catholic artefacts Charlotte had kept for sentimental reasons from her childhood, she came to a decision. She would take three holy medals of particular significance to leave along the Way at points she had chosen. The Immaculate Conception medal would be left at the start in St Jean Pied de Port; the Holy Communion medal would be placed on La Cruz de Ferro; the final, most beautiful medal of the Madonna and Child, a gift from her father's mother for her First Holy Communion, would be left in the cathedral at Santiago. Her hope was that she would be able to unburden some of the hurt and pain caused to her by her Catholic upbringing.

For those readers who may not be familiar with the concept of holy medals, perhaps we should explain a little. Little boys, back when we were young, would avidly collect cigarette cards (almost every adult smoked back then) and they would play all sorts of games to win cards for their collections. The little girls in the convent we attended, in contrast collected holy pictures and holy medals. The holy pictures were small pictures of saints, the Virgin Mary, Jesus and so forth. There was kudos in owning unusual holy pictures and a picture, gilt edged and blessed by the Pope was the trump card – not sure the avarice and gloating that ensued was entirely in keeping with Christian ideals. A similar attitude towards little holy medals prevailed. The medals were often mass-produced tin portraits of the Holy Family, but could be made of precious metals, and were often given as gifts at important Catholic feast days and on occasions such as First Holy Communion and Confirmation day.

Blog (Jane) 15 March 2013 Still Training

There has been an hiatus with this blog as I couldn't work out how people could access it -- I know - "what a "Luddite"! Anyway, I might be back on track. (Jane had a horror of the thought of strangers reading the blog so had opened it to named people only. However, this became too complicated and even the named people could only access the blog once and needed a new invitation with each new posting. So, on the basis that no one would be remotely interested in reading it anyway, the privacy settings were removed.)

C and I have now begun training properly - packed the rucksacks - about 20 lb weight - not sure that we can get it any lower; booked the air tickets and agreed the first two days; and, yes, we have done a little bit of actual walking! In fact we must have done all of four miles in the snow in Derbyshire last Sunday! We are off to do the Dales Way in two weeks - the real test before our departure! More news when I have some.

Meanwhile Henry plotted every mile of the pilgrimage drawing up a route profile comparing it to some of the places we would be familiar with. It was not clear how reassuring this was as we discovered we would be way higher than Ben Nevis, the highest mountain in the UK, as we went over the Pyrenees, as high as Grisedale Pike in the Lake District, when we ascended the Alto del Perdon and would climb up once more beyond the height of Ben Nevis when we went up to La Cruz de Ferro. Even O'Cebreiro, towards the last stage of the pilgrimage, was at the same altitude as Ben Nevis. Our altitude for most of the walk across the Meseta plateau during the middle part of the pilgrimage would be at the height of Scafell Pike, the highest mountain in England. All these calculations gave Henry some sense of organised control which offset his anxieties about us two going off on our own with limited navigational and travel experience. In addition he created a huge wall chart plotting the mountains and hills together with the approximate staging posts which would go up on the wall for Jane's granddaughters to draw on and mark where their Nanny was along her journey. Once Jane and Charlotte were on their way, the girls (then six and four) also pinned up all the postcards they received from Spain, drew in animals we texted we had seen or drew in the weather their Nonno had researched was prevalent that day. The chart worked to give them some tangible sense of what their grandma was doing and how long she would be away. Their Mum also confessed later that she thought it helped her Dad cope with Jane being away for so long; he too could tick off the days until her return. Charlotte's grandson, aged only three at the time, would also follow his Grandma's journey by taking each of his Spanish cat postcards, as they arrived from Grandma in Spain, to bed with him.

Léa and Emma's wall chart showing Charlotte and Jane on O'Cebreiro

Blog (Jane) 12 April 2013 Still in Training - The Dales Way -

Well, we now have 90 miles of Dales Way under our belts, about 45 of those carrying nearly a full Camino-weight pack!

The walk was brilliant! Amazingly cold weather, loads of wind, beautiful views, and NO rain!

We did cheat in that H had arranged a baggage carrying service so we were able to pack loads of luxuries and we could gradually increase the weight in the packs over the six days. This we did over the course of the six days – not with Camino Way kit, but with equivalent bits and pieces. We felt quite pleased that we could manage the packs (just), but it was hard work.

Start of Dales Way

Things we learnt:
1. Walking with a heavy pack is a killer on the feet; you get more blisters and aches than you would normally. It has taken a week for my feet to feel normal again. The solution to this is that we shall only walk 12 miles a day for the first two weeks of the Camino and then see if we have adapted.

2. Practise using your "she-wee" before you start walking (blokes - you don't need to know, nor do those not yet of age, nor women of a delicate disposition). It's something to do with getting the right positioning on your under-carriage, but carry a spare set of trousers just in case!

3. We will definitely use our walking poles - an absolute godsend.

4. New- born lambs in plastic raincoats are awfully sweet.

5. It easier to get over stiles if the snow drift is piled high on both sides.

Things we have yet to learn:
1. Can we manage 500 miles; will the feet/ hips/ knees cope?

2. Are we planning on carrying too much or just enough?

3. Will our light-weight water-proofs be sufficient?

4. Why are we doing this?!

Anyway -- two weeks and four days to go before we fly out on 1st May

We had put a good deal of effort into researching the best kit to take with us. We already had a fair bit but we had to get sleeping bags, big rucksacks and lightweight waterproofs. What we did have, fortunately were good boots. BUT, on The Dales Way, Charlotte had got a blister and Jane's feet had got very wet. We both, individually and separately went into a complete funk about our boots, purchasing new ones, wearing them round the house, returning them, purchasing others – all within "two-and-a-half minutes" of leaving for the walk. We knew this was ridiculous and we knew that wearing new boots for such a long walk is definitely not recommended, but that is what we ended up doing. Jane has a much wider right foot than left foot so she persuaded a local cobbler to stretch the right boot of her latest purchase on a boot stretcher just two days before departure. Then, following a tip on YouTube, she laced the right boot so that the middle section of the boot was unlaced, but the ankle and heel were well "strapped in". We were beginning to become neurotic about these boots as we had read so much about blisters and pilgrims having to take recovery rest days, seeking medical assistance, getting back and shin problems from the peculiar stance they adopted to compensate for their painful blisters and in a few cases having to give up. As it transpired we ended up with one tiny blister between us and found we had other things to worry about instead. The boots were fine.

In terms of our other pieces of kit we both got three-season sleeping bags, very light but a little bulky, together with silk liners that could be easily washed. We got Gregory Ladies 45/55L rucksacks that had an amazing shaped hip belt with a very comfortable lumbar pad and a huge expanding main opening (hence the 45/55 litre capacity) that was to prove enormously useful in the second part of the pilgrimage. We got Gortex Active cagoules that were incredibly light and windproof. We got medium sized travel towels. Little things we added were, ear-plugs and eye mask, universal sink plugs (proved to be very useful as with one tiny exception we ended up always doing our own laundry and not always in the most well-equipped of places), stretchy peg-less washing lines (invaluable), small butcher's hook for hanging stuff in showers, head-torches (used pretty much every day), foot lubricant to prevent friction, anti-bedbug pillow case plus old pillowcase from home (we had read a lot of stuff about bedbugs in the hostels). These items, together with two sets of walking trousers and tops, wet-weather over-trousers, fleece, light nightwear, minimal underwear, three sets of walking socks, sun hats, Buffs, wet-weather gloves, basic toiletries in small containers, meds, plasters, toilet paper and tissues, water bottle, Crocs, re-charger for phone, penknife, small sewing kit, notebook and pencil, tiny nylon back sack for valuables and evenings, walking poles and huge dry sack that rucksack could go in (bedbug deterrent), were all stuffed into the rucksack or worn/carried about our person. Oh yes, we also took the she-wees!

Blog (Charlotte) 30thApril. Less than twenty four hours to go. You will be pleased to see that Jane does actually have a sister called Charlotte; I came down to Sussex yesterday from Sheffield to do our final prep and then to set off tomorrow for the Camino. I am so excited and have been for weeks. It all feels more real now. We have finished packing and weighing our rucksacks and have managed minimal but sensible gear for all weathers. From the weather sites we can see that we will be needing our wet weather stuff from the start. It was Jane's idea to do the Camino and I am so glad she did as I am looking forward to spending time with her walking, talking or not, eating and drinking and (singing); we shall come back to the singing. We have both got new boots and are now trying not to obsess too much about them. We are carrying a small pharmacy of blister prevention and treatments. I shall write more when we are on the Way.

Blog (Jane): We have both received good luck cards from many people. Thank you all of you for kind thoughts -- it will buoy us up no end (and now we cannot slope off to the Costa del Sol and pick up an all-over tan without you all wanting to know how we managed that in walking gear and backpacks!). We appreciate all your good wishes.

Photo below is of the entire content of my backpack. (This doesn't include all the stuff I shall have draped around my person!) The pack will weigh in – with ½ litre of water – at approx. 21 lbs.

And (believe it or not - don't) photo number two is Charlotte's!

Next blog from The Camino Way!

Whilst Jane had initiated this adventure, prompted by the chance meeting with a former pilgrim on a walk a number of years before, both of us sisters did have our own, somewhat nebulous, reasons for embarking on such a big walk. Charlotte was retiring from a much loved job, supporting the carers of people with dementia. She had helped set up this unusual service many years before in Sheffield and since then helped train numerous other health services to deliver the support groups and counselling to carers so that they could cope better. Unfortunately, National Health Service changes had meant that her service was being significantly constrained and reduced. This together with the in-service politics was destroying the pleasure in the working environment, although the joy of working with the carers and the person they supported remained. Charlotte knew it might take her some time to adjust to retirement, but also she needed to determine how to accommodate the negative feelings that had arisen from the changes imposed on her service. A 500 mile walk might give her the time and space to think these things through.

In contrast, Jane had retired several years before, not just because she was two years the senior, but because she had to. Chronic daily headache syndrome is where an individual suffers for at least half the month with a combination of severe migraines and other severe headaches, such as tension headaches. For twelve years Jane had been under the care of a consultant neurologist and had undergone almost every conceivable drug regimen to manage the increasingly worsening headaches she suffered from. Her headaches were almost literally daily, with the very occasional month when there would be one headache-free day. Jane's job, after many years of teaching and college management, was as a senior staff member in a Government agency responsible for the planning and funding of post-16 education. It was challenging, exciting and enjoyable and very demanding. Eventually, Jane had to pass her baton on to someone else as she could no longer contribute at the frenetic level needed. The blow to self-esteem and sense of purpose was enormous. The headaches remained a dreary and frequently utterly debilitating experience, but contributing to the care of grandchildren helped plug the work gap a bit. Bizarrely walking was often one of the few things that slightly ameliorated the headaches. Deciding to walk the Camino Way, planning for the walk and doing it would perhaps help compensate for those feelings of failure and uselessness.

Neither of us sisters was embarking on this pilgrimage for religious purposes or motivations. However, we had been raised as Roman Catholics and the fact that the Way is a Catholic pilgrimage route did have resonance with us. In addition, Jane had been asked by her very elderly mother-in-law, Maria, to pray for her along the route. Maria lived with Henry and Jane and the whole family was holding its breath that Maria might reach her centenary that summer. A number of Maria's Catholic friends then asked Jane to add their loved ones in trouble to her prayer list. The family was also hoping that their very poorly sister-in-law would respond well to chemotherapy and live to see her first grandchild, due that August. Charlotte too had received requests for prayers to be said and for candles to be lit for a friend's departed partner. Despite everyone knowing we were agnostic, none-the-less these requests were made, but more strangely, we accepted them all. And not only that, we honoured them all as well!

For some people deciding to walk the Camino Way may be like deciding where to go for their next summer holiday. For others it may be a challenge on the "bucket list" to be ticked off. For yet others it may be an opportunity to get together with friends and spend time with them. Some will have seen Martin Sheen's film, "The Way", and wanted to see those sights and have those experiences themselves. Obviously for many the pilgrimage to Santiago de Compostela is one of the most revered pilgrimage routes and, therefore enormously desirable for the devout to experience, in particular if they are remembering lost loved ones, suffering poor health or giving thanks for good fortune. None of these reasons for embarking on the Camino Way is better or worse than another, just different as people's experiences and circumstances are different. For us two sisters our motivations were fuzzy: to find time to reflect on how to live in retirement, to prove we were still effective independent woman, to deliver on an ambition (we've said it, so we'll do it), but also to step away from the daily demands on us, to spend some time together, to have a brand new experience – and yes, all within an historical, but also present-day context of a pilgrimage, with echoes both comforting and disturbing from a Catholic childhood.

Henry was picking up Jane's responsibilities for after-school care of the grandchildren, whilst also looking after his frail mother and undertaking a huge drainage project in the garden. Without this support it would have been impossible for Jane to think of sloping off for five to six weeks. We had decided to do the walk in May as we had read that this was not an unduly busy time on the Camino Way as the weather was still a bit changeable, but was likely to be improving. Some, but not all of these things turned out to be true. It would not be too hot (more about that later – little did we know that the UK and Europe were about to experience one of the coldest springs in a good number of years!) and beds in hostels would be easy to come by. Our sister-in-law, Liz, was having a 60th birthday party on June 16th so we had an end-date to aim for. We had thought about walking in the autumn, but both felt that spring flowers would "top" ploughed fields as scenic company. We also thought that if we put the walk off, something might happen to prevent us going or we might just chicken out. And Jane, despite the agnosticism wanted to get those prayers said sooner rather than later.

We had both "dipped into" the Discussion Forum on the Confraternity of St James website. We had individually followed various threads: on the over-60's walking the Way; on bedbugs; on what to carry in one's pack; on blisters and how to treat them; on when best to walk; on the danger of big dogs; on personal and property security. We had looked at other people's video clips and photos and had been a little disconcerted with the road walking despite common sense telling us that over a 500 mile distance one is going to have to traverse some towns and cities. We had, elsewhere, come across adverts for baggage transport, but not for one minute did we think this relevant to the pilgrimage we were setting out on. If we thought about it at all, we thought it might be for people who did not have the luxury of doing the entire 500 mile route but had to, instead, do odd weeks here and there. I think we also thought, subliminally, that this trip was already costing us an awful lot and such a portering service would have a huge additional and unnecessary cost. We had used baggage carrying services on a number of our long-distance walks in the UK, but we had been doing long mileages and long days often with big elevations to climb up and down. Those walks had in addition, been holidays. Now we were embarking on a pilgrimage; not that we thought that pilgrimage equates to privation, just that it was different from a holiday.

So there we were: aged 62 and 60, not especially fit, with heavy packs, little real understanding of the geography of the land we would be walking through, but armed with a Spanish phrase book, John Brierley's guide book and a bucket full of bravado. May 1st 2013 we set off.

CHAPTER THREE THE ADVENTURE BEGINS

May 1st 2013 We're On Our Way

It is a long time since either of us had felt such trepidatory excitement: the butterflies in the stomach combined with exhilaration, but sprinkled with a real anxiety about whether or not we should be doing this. The rucksacks were carefully packed and weighed, everything grouped and parcelled into one of several dry sacks within the pack. The weight was well above the "no more than 10% of body weight" that is often recommended, but below the "maximum of 10 kilograms" that is also recommended. We had managed the Dales Way, we would manage this. We were, however, very glad to dump the sacks onto an airport trolley as soon as were able to.

Sussex to Stansted; Stansted to Biarritz airport – pas de problem – we were travellers who took travelling in their stride. Well, after we had collected our rucksacks at Biarritz airport, we duly got in the bus queue to take the bus to Bayonne where we were staying the night. The bus seemed awfully late according to the published timetable, but we persevered with our queuing, vaguely aware that the very extensive taxi queue on the other side of the airport entrance was only slowly decreasing. Eventually, just as we were becoming more uneasy, a young man detached himself from the taxi queue, came over and explained to us that May 1st was Labour Day in France and no buses operated on that day. He then very kindly insisted we took his place in the taxi queue. He was not a pilgrim, just an extremely kind local man who cottoned on that these foreigners had not a clue! However, although this particular Good Samaritan was not a Camino pilgrim, he had been queuing next to one – well they are pretty easy to detect as they usually have huge rucksacks on their backs. We introduced ourselves to Ingo from Germany and we all shared a taxi, eventually, into Bayonne. The business opportunity of running taxis from the airport on Labour Day seemed to have been missed by the locals; but perhaps it was just part of learning to be patient – a lesson we would come to find very useful throughout our pilgrimage.

Bayonne was a delight to wander around that first evening, but we were exhausted as one often is on travel days. The leaving home in plenty of time, all the waiting around, tearful farewells, speaking French on our arrival, the huge exciting reality that we had actually committed ourselves, all took its toll. We would eat and sleep and then catch the mid-morning train to St Jean Pied de Port the next day. However, finding somewhere to eat was not so simple as nowhere was serving before at least 7.00 pm. Little did we know that compared to Spain this was incredibly early. Once we had found an open restaurant, we went a little mad in our excitement at starting the adventure and ordered both starters and mains only to be utterly overwhelmed at the size of the starters – enough to feed a family of four – completely impossible to finish. Was this an omen? Our eyes are bigger than our stomachs; we had bitten off more than we could chew; we could start but we might not finish? Or was tiredness imbuing our actions with portent. Whatever. The lesson we learned was to be more measured.

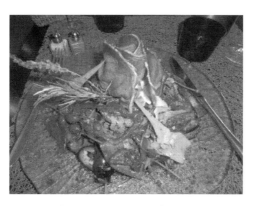

A gigantic starter in Bayonne

We had both invested in a tiny notebook with the intention of jotting down occasional noteworthy events or sightings along the way. In addition, our Brierley guidebook had periodic pages with space for one's reflections to be included. During the course of the next several weeks we would see many people occupied for considerable time writing in, what we assumed were their pilgrimage journals. We rather assumed these journals contained profound reflections of a spiritual nature, rather than a routine listing of the travel details of the day – distance travelled, food eaten, places stopped at, etc. Jane had kept a girlhood diary for a number of years when young which had been of such staggering mundaneness that even she could not bear to re-read them – far more entries of the "Washed my hair today. Still weigh too much. Steam pudding and custard for lunch at school. Yummy!" variety than entries exploring the purpose of existence or the reason why. Anyway, we both started what would become a routine throughout the journey, writing up a few thoughts at the end of most days. We shall include a few throughout this book. You might come to feel that Jane never did learn her lesson from those girlhood diaries! But at the very least the notebooks allowed us to remember when we did have "steam pudding" and whereabouts we ate it.

On 2 May we took the glorious little train from St Jean Pied de Port up through the foothills of the Pyrenees. We sedately travelled up beside cascading jungle-green rivers as the terrain became ever more steep. The train was full of other pilgrims, but all appeared to be quietly thinking about where they were and what they were doing. Given that later we would find that pilgrims could not seem to help but talk to each other, it was strange how reserved everybody was. It did not strike us as strange at the time as people always tended to keep themselves to themselves on trains, but it was indicative in retrospect of how people changed on the Camino, from being very mindful of what was one's own space to becoming less concerned about that space. We were both excited, but possibly also a little fearful as we had ahead of us the first part of our climb up the Pyrenees. It was less a question of whether or not we would manage it, more a question of how slow we would be and how much it would hurt.

Day 1. May 2nd St Jean Pied de Port – Orrison 8K/5M (stayed at private Auberge Orrison)

The Pilgrims' Office and at 14.00 setting off at last!

Clearly it takes time to become a pilgrim and we were not yet there. As trainee pilgrims we hefted our rucksacks and walked up hill from the railway station to the old town of St Jean to find the Pilgrim's Office to collect our credencials. We then immediately became annoyed to discover the Office was closed for an hour for lunch.

Now, instead of being grateful towards the volunteers who issued these essential "pilgrim passports" that would allow us to stay in the pilgrim hostels, we just felt irritated that the Office chose to close just as the train from Bayonne arrived. We were not the only ones not yet in a very "pilgrim-y" frame of mind as we were jostled and pushed by an elderly German man who clearly felt that by putting the pressure on us in the queue he would get along faster and by niftily over-taking us as we eventually went through the open door he would be served ahead of us. One of his group obviously was embarrassed by his behaviour and pulled him back to allow us forward. None of this tallied with how we thought we would feel at the real start of the pilgrimage – one could get this sort of hassle in any supermarket back home.

And then we were off. We briefly stopped at the Porte Notre Dame for the first "holy medal discarding ritual" as Charlotte cast her Immaculate Conception holy medal into the green waters of the river. We proceeded to the Route Napoleon over the top of the Pyrenees which had been opened that day after a recent closure for snow and the death of a pilgrim, possibly lost in that snow. This would mean we would not have to take the road route to Roncesvalles, our first stop in Spain the following day, but instead would be able to tackle the mountain route.

The weather had been threatening all day and now decided to deliver on its threat. In The Lake District we had learnt not to get our base and mid-layer of clothing wet before putting on a top layer, so we diligently put on all our wet-weather gear and set off once more. We then had to make decisions: did we stay prudently dry whilst carrying our heavy packs up the first part of this mountain and die of heat exhaustion or did we take the wet-weather gear off and climb the mountain, albeit a bit damp? We chose dampness. Well, by now we had been walking for about 45 minutes and had our packs off several times, undone them, rummaged through for kit, packed everything up again and moved less than a mile. At this rate we would arrive at that day's destination the following day!

We got into a rhythm eventually and began to truly enjoy the scenery around us as we left habitation below us. It was hard work and we were slow, but we had known this would be the case. What we had not bargained on was actually seeing, both near and afar, flocks of enormous Griffon Vultures, gliding and swooping above but also grazing in fields; it was like seeing something from a natural history TV programme. We had to step off the path at one point (no problem there; any excuse for a rest) to allow a herd of docile, patient, clanging cows to go past as they were moved by cowherds to higher pastures; we could almost believe for a moment that we had jumped into the children's classic story, "Heidi". We did not meet other pilgrims. We guessed that many from the mid-day train must be starting their climb the next day and possibly doing the full "up-and-over" to Roncesvalles in one go. We knew the "pushy German group" were going on the road route via Valcarlos. None-the-less, it was a little strange to see nobody. The two of us walked up at a slow and steady plod, phlegmatically accepting that around every steep hairpin bend would be yet another steep path and hairpin bend. After three or so hours we arrived, tired and very damp and had our initiation into hostel living.

Some of the cows we met with huge bells round their necks.

Arriving at Auberge Orrison

We entered a fug of a bar and spectacles immediately steamed up. It was absolutely packed. People obviously walked much faster than us or had arrived hours ago having set off after breakfast. We were congratulated on our achievement of arriving by a tall South African. We were shown to our room (you have to pre-book at this hostel) and, despite having read about dormitories on the Discussion Forum, were completely nonplussed to find a small room with three very sturdy sets of bunk beds all of which, barring two, were obviously taken. The two beds left were, of course, on the top. We immediately cottoned on that if you want a bottom bunk you have to get in early. Jane took the left, Charlotte took the right and would later learn that this was a mistake. Having draped our wet things on a chair, we decided we needed a drink more than a shower so we went outside and round to the bar. It was a delight to discover Ingo, our German taxi buddy, was also staying here.

At around 18.30, the two long refectory style tables began to fill up with pilgrims and together we enjoyed a filling, but very delicious communal pilgrim's meal with platters put down at intervals along the tables and whoever was sitting nearest serving the people around them. Everybody chatted to the people nearby in whatever language they could muster. After the Torta de Santiago course was cleared we were all then asked to stand up and introduce ourselves, say where we were from, where we were hoping to get to and why. We two were the only British pilgrims and were surprised at the number of Canadians present. Two of these Canadians were awesome: two seventy year old ladies who had already walked 740 kilometres from Le Puy in France and intended to get to Fisterra after walking to Santiago, a further 900 kilometres approximately. They were enormously inspirational to us as they appeared to be ordinary older women, not lean as whippets or ostentatiously athletic. If they could have achieved so much already and were still game for yet more, we both believed our pilgrimage would be achievable. We were to meet up with Susie and Cecelia several times in the weeks ahead. There were quite a number of German pilgrims, two from Brazil, one from South Africa, some French and Irish; in total there were eleven nationalities present. After this pleasant evening, everyone departed for early beds.

Now we met our room companions properly: two very chatty Irish women, Lily and Claire, and two charming Canadian men, Bill and Leo. We had our showers and set up our beds putting over the mattress the paper sheet provided for purposes of hygiene. We were to regret not taking this paper sheet with us after we left as many other hostels did not provide them and were not always as clean. This was our introduction to how we managed the simple activities of preparing for the night: what to take into the tiny shower cubicle with us and how to keep those things dry; where the timer light switch was so that we could cope when plunged into the dark mid-shower; how to secrete our valuables within our bed space and where on earth to put our specs so we could find them but not crush them when asleep.

One of the Irish women, Lily, had the tiniest sleeping bag and what looked like a day sack hooked on the back of her bed. How could she manage to be so minimalist? We two were beginning to suffer from an ailment that did not leave us for a number of weeks – rucksack envy. She said that her friends were all amazed at how she managed to pack everything into a sack so small, yet Jane had seen with her own eyes a largish cosmetics-cum-toiletries bag, so we wondered as well how she managed with the tiny sack. All would be revealed in the week ahead when we saw Lily and her companion ahead of us one day with Lily looking like the proverbial Irish Tinker with her sack festooned with dangling accoutrements, including a large, snazzy handbag. Well, we could all have small rucksacks if half the content is draped on the outside!

And so to bed. Well, we went to bed, but barely went to sleep. Charlotte quickly discovered the big problem with the right hand top bunk: there was a huge low wooden beam running along the side of the room under which the bunk was located. If she lay flat on her back she was OK. If she lay on her side she would become wedged in between the bed and the beam. If she tried to sit up she would concuss herself. So it had to be sleeping flat on her back with the occasional attempt to sleep on her side but right at the furthermost edge of the bunk where there was no over-shadowing beam. To make the most of it Charlotte laid out her specs, watch and head-torch on this unlooked for beam and zipped up her sleeping bag and hoped for the best. Well, the best was a little illusive. I do not know about you, Dear Reader, but our normal night time habits were to get up once at the most for a bathroom visit during the night. This night became the first of very many nights to follow when this usual nightly routine was completely thrown out of the window. Whether it was something to do with anxiety, or an early bed after supper, or perhaps there was something in the water, but that night and for numerous nights thereafter we had to get up several very inconvenient times. OK, nobody wants to get out of a warm bed into the cold. However, extricating oneself quietly from a mummy-shaped sleeping bag, wriggling to the ladder, getting down the ladder, not treading on the sleeper in the bottom bunk, shuffling around to find Crocs to put on one's feet, locating the door in the pitch dark, finding the corridor timer light, visiting the not entirely delightful loo, and then repeating most of this palaver to get back up into one's bunk and bag was a nightmare.

There was an added conundrum. Jane was very concerned that first night with issues of security. We had read on the Discussion Forum that pilgrims must keep their valuables with them at all times, even in the shower; a matter of not tempting fate. So what does one do for the several night time trips to the loo? We had each put all our valuables into a small nylon sack, which when walking we kept in our rucksacks, but which could be easily removed if we had to leave the rucksack anywhere. In these small sacks we had our money-wallet and money, passport and other necessary documents, phone and charger, drugs/medication, credencial and small purse. Jane had stuffed her small sack to the bottom of her sleeping bag – an incredibly uncomfortable arrangement and not one to be repeated. As none of our bedroom companions had looked as if they possessed the inclination to relieve us of our valuables, leave alone the "Spider Man" secret powers to silently climb up to find said valuables, it seemed sensible to leave them in the bed. We were to learn, much later, that a Korean girl did have her money stolen from her bunk whilst she was in the shower in an entirely different hostel. Suffice to say, by the time morning came we had used up so much nervous energy and slept so little, that the prospect of completing the climb over the Pyrenees was quite daunting.

Journal reflections (Jane): Simply consumed by the many practicalities of getting the train, waiting for the Pilgrim Office to open, being jostled by an impatient elderly German, getting our credencials, choosing a shell, finding somewhere to purchase food, setting off, changing into then out of wet-weather gear, the long slog up to Orrison, the confusion of mixed communal living, not sleeping a wink. My main "reflection" is that I am desperately, tearfully missing Henry and I must be mad to be doing this!

Journal reflections (Charlotte): I was very anxious as we approached St Jean. I don't want to let Jane down, but I'm worried I haven't built my strength up enough. However, six miles in I did feel more confident though my pack felt heavy on my lower back. It felt symbolic and right to drop my medal into the river at St

Jean. I had felt angry at the German man who had pushed in at the Pilgrims'
Office, but Jane said "let it go" and I did. Terrible night with very little sleep –
why? Am I anxious about today? Can I manage the pack? Am I up to all this?
I am feeling so disorganised and not in the rhythm of the Way.

Day 2. May 3rd Orrison – Roncesvalles `7.1K/10.7M (stayed at huge monastery albergue)

Route Napoleon   *Albergue at Roncesvalles*

In the morning our night time companions, together with most of
the other pilgrims at this hostel made organised and swift departures
and set off up the mountain. We two, in contrast, seemed to take
forever to get packed, breakfasted and, rather blearily, to embark on
this next significant stage of the pilgrimage. The sky was grey and
rolls of mist could be seen in the valleys below. We started once
more to climb up and up.

Looking back down where we had been

The valley mist very speedily caught up with us, the weather descended and we were surrounded by cold, wet clouds. As we began to climb we were joined by Darren, the young South African from the previous evening. Although much younger than us, he was happy to walk at our pace for the company. Darren was reluctant to go over the top on his own. We had probably all read too much about people getting lost on this mountain and certainly the weather conditions were conducive to all sorts of worrisome scenarios. As the temperature dropped we two made "beanie" hats out of our buffs and wore all our layers, but even so it was very cold, despite the heat we were generating through climbing. Poor Darren was suffering a complete shock from the contrast in temperature between the top of a European mountain and his native country and ended up digging out some socks to use as gloves. It was not practical to stop for rest breaks as we immediately got very cold so we just plodded on stopping for the odd photo opportunity, for example, as we crossed into Spain into the misty province of Navarre.

As the day wore on other pilgrims would rise up out of the mist and pass us by. These folk must have left very early in the morning from St Jean Pied de Port as we had been almost the last to leave Orrison. We had been looking out for the statue of the Virgin Mary, a landmark site on our route, but it was completely hidden in the mist so we passed it by not noticing. It threw us a bit as we knew we had a significant climb after the statue so we kept thinking we had far further to go to reach the summit than in fact we did. It was a pleasant surprise when we finally got to the top. There were heaps of snow on all sides, but clearly it had melted significantly from the path. We paused briefly outside a stinking little shepherd's hut that sheep (and perhaps others too) had clearly long used as a toilet. There was a mattress and blanket on an elevated platform, so if one was desperate and had no sense of smell, one could hole up here for a bit. As we began to descend from the summit we came to a small woodland with the path at its edge. In the broad gulley between the woodland and the fence had collected what felt like decades" worth of leaves. It felt like walking on a children's bouncy castle, quite extraordinary.

The first of many shrines we would see.

The climb up the route Napoleon and then down was hard work, especially with the heavy packs on our backs, but it was perfectly do-able; no technical difficulty. We had climbed enough Lake District peaks to know we just had to keep plodding on and that, over time, we would build stamina. This would transpire to be only partly true for us on this huge journey.

We had been told at the Pilgrim's Office that whilst the Route Napoleon had been opened that day, the descent to Roncesvalles through the beach wood was not permitted as the recent snow had made that route very dangerous. We had instead to go on the zig-zag path to Ibaneta, a slightly longer route. The descent was straight forward, but almost as soon as Jane had crossed into Spain the sore throat that had been niggling all morning became far worse and the muggy head was building up to a migraine. By the time we arrived at the enormous albergue at Roncesvalles in early afternoon, both of us were exhausted, cold, and very confused about where to go and what to do. Jane was also feeling very nauseous and knew that to arrest a full blown migraine she needed to take drugs and lie down.

As time went by we would become familiar with the varied routines of arrival at hostels but this time we had not realised the protocol was to remove one's boots and store them in the boot room before going to the reception desk. We were soon corrected. The hostel was run by Dutch volunteers, but none seemed to have any English that day and we certainly had no Dutch. We both registered and were allocated bunk numbers, but the reception volunteer had unwittingly turned over two pages in between allocating each of our bunks, thus we were several bunk bays apart. Once we were shown to our bunks (in bays of two bunks/four beds) it was clear there was no one else in Jane's bay but Charlotte's was full with a French party who wanted her bed for a friend arriving later so were not especially welcoming of her. Jane just had to collapse with some migraine and anti-sickness drugs whilst Charlotte endeavoured to resolve the problem by asking for a simple reallocation of bunk numbers at the reception. Well – not simple at all – once numbers are allocated they cannot be changed, no matter how much Charlotte explained that we are sisters walking together, one is ill and there is no one else in that bay. Charlotte stuck to her guns and eventually a kindly American volunteer came over and immediately changed the bunk allocation – so, it could have been simple from the outset.

After a sleep for a couple of hours and a shower, Jane felt well enough to foray out. However, Charlotte then realised she could not find her watch. Everything had to be unpacked and searched through. She had to return to the French bunk encampment and search there, and in the showers. No watch. Then she realised that it must still be sitting on that visually picturesque, but horribly inconvenient wooden beam above the bunk bed at the Orrison auberge where she had placed it for safety the previous night. . Ah well, perhaps another lesson on the Way was not to be too attached to one's possessions. We went out to see what Roncesvalles had to offer. We took our cagoules as the weather was still threatening although not actually raining. We booked a pilgrim's meal for the evening at a place nearby and then found a bar to have a much needed coffee. On returning to the albergue Jane did some minimal laundry in the vast wash room on the ground floor. The facilities at this albergue were first class and very clean; we even had lockable lockers at the ends of our bunks. We now had two other companions in our bunk bay; above Jane was Luca, a young Italian boy and above Charlotte a very jet-lagged Brazilian who wanted our help in deciding which clothes to jettison from his pack as it was way too heavy.

As we set off for our evening meal, Jane decided to take her cagoule despite it only being a short distance, none-the-less it was cold. Charlotte went back for hers, but no cagoule could be found. Once more the unpacking and searching routine commenced, but this time with a significant degree of panic as it was very clear that wet-weather gear and warmth were needed on this journey; it would be hugely difficult to continue without this sort of protection and we had no idea where we might purchase another jacket. After some considerable time with both of us going over the same places and same bags we remembered the bar and fair charged round there – on the back of the chair Charlotte had been sitting on was her jacket, where she had left it. Neither of us could believe how "dappy" we both were and resolved to try and get better organised and at least to check and double check whenever we moved on from a stop or a rest. Eventually we got to the hotel where we had booked to eat. All our room companions from the previous night were at the same communal table as us for our evening meal together with a number of other pilgrims. There was much lively chat.

Journal reflections (Jane): Whilst I felt an enormous sense of achievement and relief to have completed the Route Napoleon over the Pyrenees, I also felt ill today and felt as I have so frequently in the past that I have to put a brave and sociable face on when it's the last thing I want to do. It was lovely walking with Darren, but it did mean having to be sociable and upbeat. The company in the evening was fun, but some people were too overbearing and left little room for quieter folks and this was the case with some very vivacious members of the table seemingly intent on making their light shine ever brighter. Perhaps my irritation was because I felt unwell and had consumed too many migraine drugs; perhaps I should learn to be less judgemental of others; perhaps it just takes all sorts ... Still tomorrow will be, as Henry frequently says once we've got to the top of a hill, "downhill all the way!"

Journal reflections (Charlotte): Felt very fatigued as we walked in the mist, but as I progressed I felt "we can do this". We met many familiar faces from Orrison. I am loving the camaraderie. I have lost my watch; maybe it is a message I should not be ruled by time nor let it dictate what I should be doing.

Blog (Jane) 3rd May   The Route Napoleon - Hola

Hi Everyone! This is just a short blog to let you all know we are alive and well (ish) - I have caught a cold (I think it is a French one as I could feel it before we crossed the frontier! Definitely "un rhume".) We are coping fine but are very discombobulated. We constantly cannot find anything and keep losing bits (and finding them). Today it was Charlotte's wrist watch then later her beautiful jacket from Mark (left in a bar but still there when we retraced our steps). I am sure we shall get into the swing of things, but sharing mixed dormitories with just a few loos is not within my comfort zone at the moment.

We have met, chatted to and dined with some nice people. We are utterly exhausted today having climbed over the Pyrenees in the mist and rain. It was very cold on the top and really you just had to trudge on as sitting and resting just made you very cold.

I am down to just a few minutes on the pay computer so I'll quickly try and add a photo. If nothing appears it means I ran out of time before I could fathom how to do it. (No joy on this occasion – better luck next time.)

We both slept a bit better that night in our broad, comfortable bottom bunks that we could actually sit up in, although Jane's cold had got to the streaming-like-a-tap phase. The lights went out automatically at 22.30 and we lay listening to the cacophony of small noises that are inevitable when about eighty people are sleeping in the same huge room. The lights would come on again automatically at 06.00, but long before this Luca, above Jane, had got up and incredibly quietly and swiftly got himself packed up and left at 05.15. Others elsewhere on our floor followed suit (there were a number of floors full of pilgrims, stacked like sardines). Long before the lights came on the dormitory was alive with comings and goings, rucksack packing and ablutions. We were much better organised in our packing and after a brief breakfast of yesterday's left over picnic, we were out on the road by 07.40. We were just beginning to get an inkling of an idea that perhaps the month of May was not the quiet month we had believed it would be on the Camino Way.

CHAPTER FOUR   DISCOMBOBULATION

Day 3. May 4th Roncesvalles – Zubiri 21.9K/13.7M (stayed in a private pension, Goikoa)

It was damp and misty and cold as we set off from Roncesvalles with most of our layers on but with joy in our hearts as we knew we had tackled and managed the Napoleon Route over the Pyrenees. Nothing would be as hard as that, or so we thought. We would find there are all sorts of hard.

Leaving Roncesvalles in the mist

As we walked the mist began to recede and we bumped into Bethany, a lovely American woman walking without a pack. She told us that the Pilgrim's Office had advised her not to attempt to carry her huge pack over the Route Napoleon as it was way too heavy. She had then arranged to get it transported to Zubiri where she was hoping she could send some things home to Hawaii. We suggested that she bought some walking poles which would help take the weight of her pack off her knees and hips. Bethany explained that she, like us the previous day, had gone to the bar in Roncesvalles for a much needed refreshment, but had only that morning realised she had left her lovely new walking poles in the bar. She had rushed along immediately but the bar was well and truly shut with no one answering her urgent knocks on the door. She could not loiter for too long on the off chance the proprietor opened up and that the poles were still there, so she cut her losses and set off. It makes one think that if we and Bethany were remotely typical of new pilgrims, that bar could do a very good business in the re-sale of almost-new pilgrim gear.

Walking from Roncesvalles to Zubiri

Well, not withstanding Henry's optimistic view that when one is at the top of a mountain, it is then downhill all the way, in fact there was a considerable amount of uphill on the walk down the far side of the Pyrenees. We were cottoning on that "Alto" in our guide book map meant hill! We stopped in a little town, Burguete, to buy provisions and to admire the deep channels on each side of the road that took away the mountain snow melt. Apart from the one shop which was open to capitalise on the exodus of pilgrims from Roncesvalles in the early morning, all was closed and silent – this would be the case for the vast majority of our morning exits in the weeks to come. After a cold and misty start, the sun came out and we walked on a clear path through beautiful woodland. As the day wore on we took off layers and put on sun hats; Charlotte even unzipped the bottom part of her trouser legs – not something that was going to happen too many more times. In the process of removing her trouser legs, Charlotte felt that the roll of tissues in the pocket felt a little strange. On investigating, low and behold she discovered her wrist watch that she had believed would forever grace the beam in the hostel at Orrison! She had simply put it in a safe place, but we were too early in the journey to have memorised all the safe places for different things. We were glad that we had this tangible evidence that we were managing our significant discombobulation – the sense of being out of control and confused. It was a lovely walk, but after eight hours we were utterly exhausted as we approached Zubiri, our destination.

We crossed the ancient bridge into the town and were immediately accosted by a Spanish lady, who on learning we had no hostel booked, practically dragged us to her pension. At 30 euros for the two of us it was pricier than a hostel but we wanted a little personal space after only two nights of dormitory dwelling. Later we bumped into Canadian Bill, from our first night in Orrison, who advised us that all the lodgings in Zubiri were full so we were grateful for our importunate Spanish lady with her high rise rooms. As it transpired our room, whilst six floors up, was clean and comfortable, but there was only one bathroom/toilet for nine people, two of whom were teenage girls, a species never known for its speed in the bathroom. This was a problem for Jane as her old ailment of irritable bowel syndrome, originally triggered by one of her migraine medicines, appeared to be returning – not a good state of affairs when there are limited and shared toilets and fairly open pathways on the route. Hey ho – the trials of a pilgrim!

Top floor lodgings at Zubiri

We ate a pilgrim menu with Canadians Bill and Leo and a number of others and had an unpleasant encounter with a barman who tried to rook us over change for drinks – tried the same thing with some Americans later, so we think it was him and not us and hoped he was not typical of Spanish barmen. Charlotte had stood her ground and retrieved her rightful change and we were then beckoned over by a group of pilgrims. We would become used to joining groups of strangers who would reveal details of their lives. The woman in this group had become lost in the mist on the Pyrenees and was discovered by one of the Australian men at the table as she was praying aloud for help. Her rucksack was huge and she was not a tiny woman. We hoped she would make it all the way.

Journal reflection (Jane): Socialness on the Way is de rigueur so if you're not up for it, it can be a little tricky. Had a chat with Henry who phoned to check all was well – felt tearful and homesick.

Journal reflection (Charlotte): Had a dreadful night, becoming so anxious about my ability to look after Jane (not well) – I know it's daft as she is perfectly able to look after herself.

We had been given advice from people at home, including a physiotherapist, on how to look after ourselves and in particular our leg muscles throughout the trip. We daily applied a lubricant to our feet before putting on our socks. We also applied arnica gel to our shins before walking and anti-inflammatory gel when the day's walk was complete. As time went by we applied the arnica and anti-inflammatory gel to hips, lower-back and shoulders as well. It seemed to work as the vast majority of mornings we woke up ready to go again. So the following morning when we had completed the battle for the bathroom and after a poorly night for Jane, we had a communal breakfast with our house mates and were happy to get going. At breakfast we met a quirky French lady in late middle age who talked much but whose name escaped us. Jane was the only one who had a bit of French at the table, but this did not deter this lady from conversing continuously and at speed with everybody – in loud French. We were to meet her a few times in the period ahead when at all times she appeared to almost skip along, darting from one side of the path to the other collecting bits and pieces and decorating the many columns of stones that pilgrims leave along the way. She was like a little magpie bird darting hither and thither. If she had been English we would have called her eccentric.

Day 4. May 5ᵗʰ Zubiri – Pamplona   21.3K/13.3M (stayed at Hotel Puerta del Camino)

After passing an enormous sprawling and ugly mineral factory just outside of Zubiri, the walk was then largely through pleasant country in fine weather. This day was the day we first became consciously aware of the little jaunty phrase, "buen camino", said by all as we pilgrims passed each other. The weather had improved, the sun was shining, the Way was busy. Perhaps everybody was beginning to feel they were on their pilgrimage proper and we were all adopting this pilgrim greeting as we adapted to our new ways of living and walking. It was not only the pilgrims who said "buen camino", but it was also the locals – particularly older folk – it confirmed this walk was qualitatively different to just any old long trek.

One of the many bridges crossed

It was clear to Jane that her tummy problem was getting worse so she texted Henry to ask him to book a hotel room in Pamplona, which he did. It was such a relief to know we had a place in the city and would not have to share limited bathroom facilities whilst in a delicate condition. We probably both had a bit of an anxiety about the cities on our route, despite the fact that Charlotte was the city girl whilst Jane was the country mouse. It was something to do with their busy-ness and also to do with security. When we had done the Dales Way as part of our preparations, we stayed in the home of a young family who let out two of their rooms for bed and breakfast. We asked if they ever worried about the security of all their lovely things with strangers coming and going. They said that it was only Dales Way walkers who passed their house and stayed; they were largely a particular group of walkers, middle-aged and middle-class, who mostly carried all their gear, so from a practical perspective and a "type of walker" perspective were very unlikely to steal. It was much the same on the Camino where it was just pilgrims passing by – pilgrims would be unlikely to steal from each other and anyway, would then have to carry the ill-gotten goods. Cities were different.

The end of the day's walk involved an almost five kilometre plod through the built up areas from Trinadad de Arre onwards. we finally arrived at the delightful walled city of Pamplona. We found it quite exhausting walking through these suburbs as, from a point of courtesy, we did not use our walking poles. On earth or gravel paths the poles made very little noise, but on pavements they click-clacked loudly. We only truly appreciated the benefit of the poles in taking weight off our backs during the occasions we did not or could not use them! It was bliss to be shown up to our delightful en-suite room!

We were a little nonplussed to read the notices in the room that had pages of warnings to guests not to open the door to anyone, not to leave anything of the remotest value in sight, to leave anything of real value at the reception desk, and so forth – it was all a little OTT – was Pamplona really so vulnerable to planned hotel thievery? As we were carrying the minimum, all our stuff was of value to us, so we assumed the hotel was being ultra-cautious for insurance purposes and left everything where we dumped it. We luxuriated in our beautiful bathroom and the lovely little golf-ball shaped soap lasted us for laundry purposes for the rest of the pilgrimage! We strung up our laundry on our stretchy, no-pegs line and went out to hit the town. In the foyer we met Ayn (pronounced Ann) and Michael from California. They were briefly staying at the hotel whilst Ayn recovered from hospital treatment having been taken ill on the road to Cizur Menor. They were desperate to continue their pilgrimage and hoped to give it a try the following day. They recommended all sorts of places to visit, so off we set.

We were thrilled to find the Plaza de Toros with its amazing statues depicting the running with the bulls - the encierro. We had a much needed beverage outside Ernest Hemingway's favourite bar and sat and watched the large, happy family groups all out celebrating Mother's Day and all dressed up to the nines.

Blog (Jane) Sunday, 5 May 2013 Out of the mist and into the sun!

Four days in and we've stayed in one hotel, one small mixed dorm (ON THE TOP BUNKS!!!!!), one huge hostel, but in bays of two bunks (we shared our beds with a young Brazilian man and an even younger Italian man -- to be honest, we felt like their grannies!), a pension (one loo for 9 people) and now we are in a lovely hotel in Pamplona with our very own bath (I'm not sure I can get Charlotte out of it!)

We have done a lot of very varied walking, on roads, on tracks, up hills (very big ones), along rivers, over bridges. Spain is a bit like a beautiful summer Lake District with a touch of winter thrown in at the beginning. Our bods are staying OK at the moment and we are getting used to the packs (Sheelagh and Angela thanks so much for your contribution to getting me fit enough to do this.) My language skills keep deserting me, but I have used French and a little Italian (thanks to Madeleine), Spanish is another question; thank goodness that English is now the new lingua franca.

Blog (Charlotte): We have had an adventurous time getting emotionally and physically into the Camino Way zone, so many things to think about at first but some are now becoming habits. We are better at packing our rucksacks and hitting the road (the fact is we do then have to stop to take off our, fleece, jacket, or shake out a boot again.) Henry is well used to our way of walking. Today, Sunday, we really did get into a good rhythm and covered miles with some pace but not overstretching our bodies.

We have enjoyed the spring flowers and the scent of pine resin and earth drying as the temperature rises and the sun shines, butterflies emerging and swifts, swallows and house martins swooping, huge birds of prey migrating across the country.

There is a strong Camino camaraderie amongst us all and we are enjoying meeting up with fellow travellers we have met before.

Blog (Jane):- A bit of bull

This evening we explored Pamplona a little and found Plaza de Toros. We sat at Ernest Hemingway's favourite bar and caught the evening sun. The world and his wife were out. Lots of little girls in long white, first holy communion type dresses and little boys in sailor suits.

Pamplona is a walled city and seems to be surrounded by mountains.

The statue in Plaza de Toros

The receptionist at the hotel could not have been more helpful, a charming Spanish man, who, despite a misunderstanding with Henry's booking allowed us to have a pilgrim-priced dinner and breakfast. He also showed us how to use the hotel's WIFI computer so we could update our blog. Now, whilst we were appreciative of this gentleman's charm and assistance, we were not surprised as this was the usual manner, in our experience, for most staff meeting and greeting paying guests. We were to find on several future occasions that some Spanish service sector staff appear not to have been trained in the "customer knows best, we are here to serve the customer" school of hospitality training. This was not such an issue or surprise in the tiny places that must sometimes get weary of the continuous stream of pilgrims passing through. We appreciated that pilgrims must sometimes be a mixed blessing. However, it was a puzzle in the bigger towns and cities as all services must surely to some extent have to compete for and attract custom. It was startling when it came to places that advertised themselves as "tourist information centres"; but more of that later.

Journal reflection (Jane):I am enormously glad to be with my sister on this adventure. I think I would be very lonely without companionship and decision making would be far more difficult. All my silly little ill-health complaints would be far less easy to manage and cope with without someone I knew and who cared for me being there. In cities it is far less clear who are pilgrims and who are ordinary citizens – although footwear is usually a give-away. If travelling alone, one would have to sit by oneself or ask to join other people who were obviously pilgrims. I think for many men this would be less of a problem. I am very reserved and quite shy, which can be taken for unfriendliness. I suspect I would end up experiencing much solitary leisure time. Perhaps this would not be a bad thing; many people do the Camino Way alone for the precise reason of being solitary and I have no problem with my own company. However, it is lovely to share delights with another person. I am not sure that the accompanying song of the cuckoo is quite as delightful if heard only by oneself, or the animated statue of young and old men running from individually furious bulls is quite as glorious if one cannot discuss its merits with a companion. Suffice to say I am glad Charlotte agreed to accompany me despite her not having fully cleared her chest infection.

Journal reflection (Charlotte): Having feared entering a city and how it would feel not being on the Way, I have really enjoyed staying in Pamplona but look

58

forward to re-joining the Way. I am feeling confident about arranging my things and packing efficiently. My cough is annoying, but my body feels good – all intact.

Up to arriving in Pamplona we had, whilst feeling excited to be on our adventure, also felt very disconcerted. We had not expected to feel so "out of our comfort zone". We were beginning to get used to packing our rucksacks in a specific order so we could find things easily en route and we were getting the hang of the daily laundry routine. The annoying ill-health (Jane's cold, migraines and tummy problem and Charlotte's continued hacking cough) were a nuisance and a constraint. Thus, after only four days, Pamplona became one of the watersheds for us as we made several decisions. We decided we would give ourselves permission to step on and off the Way: in cities we would step off the Way and become tourists and everywhere else we would be peregrinas – pilgrims. We decided we would build in more rest days if we needed to – we had already planned to have rest breaks at Burgos and Leon. So, by the end of day four of our pilgrimage, although not "combobulated" yet, we were not quite as totally discombobulated as we had been for the first few days.

CHAPTER FIVE BEDDING DOWN

Day 5. May 6th Pamplona – Uterga 17.4K/10.9M (stayed in Camino del Perdon albergue)

We really felt as if we were getting into the swing of living as pilgrims today as we set off at 07.45 to walk through the very pleasant suburb area to leave Pamplona. It was a glorious day and although a bit cold, we started off optimistically in our shirt sleeves – our optimism would prove to be justified.

Leaving Pamplona

With all the passing references to colds, coughs, tummy problems and migraines in the first part of this book, we must sound like two whinging hypochondriacs creaking our way through the early stages of this long pilgrimage. In fact we felt quite strong and we knew that we tended to feel stronger after the first couple of hours. We were both used to a "soldiering on" mentality so whilst the health issues were real they were just another logistical conundrum to be dealt with much like determining what to do for lunch, which way to go when signs were unclear, where to aim for that day and so forth. We were also discovering that a café con leche was a very restorative beverage. We were both ardent tea drinkers but we had agreed to foreswear tea for the duration of the pilgrimage as it was unlikely that we would be able to buy or make a decent cup of English/Yorkshire tea whilst in Spain.

We were aiming for Uterga this day as we were trying to walk around 12 miles or about 20 kilometres a day. The intention was to build up stamina and extend the distance we covered each day as we got stronger. We knew we had to climb the 800 metre Alto del Perdon (the Hill of Forgiveness), although we were part-way up to start. If we were to walk to the village beyond Uterga it would add almost another five kilometres with no guarantee of a bed as there was only one modest private hostel there. We had looked at all these over-night stay options and possibilities prior to embarking on the pilgrimage, using the details in our guide book. Many pilgrims decided on a daily basis where they would stop and how far they would walk depending on how they felt each day. In contrast we had decided to be cautious in our first two weeks as our preparatory walk in the Yorkshire Dales had taught us our usual 14 – 15 miles (around 24 kilometres) a day would be very difficult to achieve with our full packs. We had, therefore planned provisional stopping places within a range of 11 – 14 miles. This pre-planning may have removed an element of spontaneity, but it also removed anxiety about where we would stop. We knew, also that we might not be able to get into hostels if we arrived late and would, therefore have to continue walking to the next place. We did not think we had the stamina to do that yet and this encouraged a cautious approach to our daily mileage ambition. So that day we set out knowing that after the climb it was a relatively short walk down to our day's end-point.

Once we had completed the road-side walking out of Pamplona and through Cizur Menor, we moved into the country side proper. Earlier we had walked off route to find a café in Cizur Menor. This in itself was a big decision as adding any additional mileage was a big deal, but it was necessary for a pre-climb coffee fix and to visit the ladies. Now, we do not have a fixation with bathrooms and toilets (although Jane's immediate family might disagree with that), but such facilities do become a bit of a bigger deal in the pilgrimage context. We were beginning to wonder why the Spanish authorities along the pilgrim route did not provide public amenities in the towns and villages. Where there were bars one could order a drink and use the facilities, but otherwise pilgrims had to use their initiative – and there was plenty of evidence behind bushes and trees of that initiative having been used by the many passing pilgrims – not a pleasant addition to the scenic wonders.

It was on the stretch from Cizur Menor to the lower slopes of Alto del Perdon that we first heard and then saw the sparklingly vibrant little Yellow Wagtail. It was completely oblivious of us, perched in a nearby bush and singing its heart out. We were to see quite a number of these delightful little birds, singly and in pairs, over the next few weeks. They would swoop in over the fields and perch and sing on the bushes on the field edges. Perhaps they were not oblivious to us afterall – perhaps they were telling us, melodiously, to clear off their patch. One of the true delights of walking in the country side is that sense of being close to nature. Because one is traveling so slowly, one sees and hears so much more than if one is on a bike or in a car. When there is no need to pack in huge distances and thus walk fast, one can stop and listen and look and smell. We took many breaks, sometimes short stops for a drink of water, sometimes longer for a snack. These breaks allowed us to look around and stare at the detail of the large and small aspects of the scenery – it almost took us back to childhood where one is down there in the grass looking at the minutiae hidden from the adult world. As grandmas we revisited that childhood world crawling around on carpets or on the grass in parks seeing the world through our grandchildren's eyes, but this walk was also giving us another opportunity to be re-introduced to the natural world in a very sensory way.

There were many pilgrims on the route that day as we began our slow ascent. The temperature was getting warmer and we needed many breaks for water. We noticed people passing with very small packs and confused these brisk pilgrims for ultra-lightweight packers – we would later realise that many pilgrims used a baggage carrying service.

We saw a very disabled pilgrim slowly making his way up the hill. He was accompanied by a young woman who carried her pack and another pack on her front. We were very impressed – at his determination and at her strength and kindness. We saw this little party on a number of occasions in the days ahead – the disabled gentleman being "supported" by different people at different times and a relief car picking them all up at the end of their day's walk. At one busy point mid-way up the Alto del Perdon we came to a memorial bench, shrine and tree. We had seen memorials first as we crossed over the Pyrenees, but clearly this was another spot where people left cards and thoughts. Jane was completely overcome after reading a brass memorial plaque to a twelve year old boy from his mummy and had to sit on the bench and publically weep (and then get cross as other pilgrims arrived and plonked all their gear all over the little memorials). The weeping was probably as much to do with the exposure of nerves and sensibilities to the many strange experiences of the past few days as it was to the pathos of the little boy's memorial.

We stopped for water; we stopped for snacks; we stopped to adjust boot tension, but we got to the top and were so grateful that we had accomplished this on such a beautiful day. Whilst the views were hazy, we did have views – so different from the white-out on the Pyrenees. There is a hugely satisfying feeling when one can look back and down at what one has achieved.

There was a slightly festive atmosphere at the top. The dominant feature was the long metal art installation depicting a row of twelve very individual pilgrims battling into the wind and striding along the edge of the hill. Behind and above these metal pilgrims loomed a row of wind turbines which seemed surprisingly appropriate in this place – the new juxtaposed with the old but with the natural power of the wind influencing both. We sat and ate our lunch sandwich and people-watched. The pilgrimage is a fascinating opportunity to observe others – although we must confess we had not yet (would we ever?) jettisoned our propensity to form opinions about (judge!)

those people. For example, on this occasion a group of Americans arrived with relatively small day sacks and much loud talk. One of the party - a portly chap, had so much long-lens photographic equipment strung around his neck that together with his Dickensian "corporation" it was a wonder he did not fall flat on his face. In his group was a small woman who promptly on arriving at the top began to do ostentatious leg stretches and side-bends whilst giving advice to someone with their boots off on the best way to manage foot care. It was all well-intentioned – just a bit loud. However, we would be very grateful to this lady as before she set off downhill, she made such a to-do about changing the ends of her walking poles over from rubber ends to the normal spike end that Jane asked her where she had got the rubber ends – she had bought them in an outdoors shop back home. Now we realised it was possible to get rubber ends for our poles we decided we would keep our eyes open – the long walk out of the centre of Pamplona that morning not using our poles had been hard work. In addition to the arriving and departing pilgrims there were two enterprising refreshment vendors on this summit – one appeared to have carried his cans of cola and orange up the hill, the other had arrived in a van and was selling coffee from his boot. After our lunch break Henry's maxim was to become true – downhill all the way!

The metal pilgrims on Alto del Perdon and Wind turbines above the summit

For Jane downhills were not too much of a problem but for Charlotte they put a strain on her knees. On these occasions Jane would stride ahead and loiter periodically waiting for Charlotte to slowly catch up. It was not a problem as there was always some lovely flora to observe or pieces of pilgrim artwork to add to. For everyone downhills take a different toll to uphills as other muscle groups are used. In addition one has to be more careful about where to place feet on the descent as one is probably moving faster and could turn an ankle or topple over – walking poles are a brilliant additional pair of "legs" in these conditions.

We arrived at the albergue in Uterga and negotiated two bunk beds from a very brusque receptionist. This same lady was charming later when serving a delicious pilgrims' menu meal in the evening, but on our arrival she was clearly feeling very harassed. We were shown our bunks in a dormitory of around sixteen people. Despite being fairly early there were only a few beds left – ours were on the top. It was becoming clear that there must be a goodly amount of competition amongst the suppliers of pilgrimage-related goods to hostel owners. We had yet to sleep in similar bunks twice. That night's bunks were of a fairly insubstantial metal frame variety with a ladder built into the frame. It was almost impossible to climb the metal ladder without shoes as the rungs dug into one's bare foot painfully. In addition, the whole bunk edifice wobbled around worryingly as we climbed up. Charlotte decided it would be easier to use a chair to help her get up. There were merits to these unstable beds, however: the surrounding bars were useful for clipping our dry sacks to, containing wash gear, the spare clothes, etc. and these particular beds were each against a wall so we could put all our bits and pieces on the wall side for safety. The last person into the dorm was a chap about our age who was allocated the last top bunk in the centre of the room – so nowhere to put his stuff except the floor. We were at the beginning of what would become a pattern – the younger one is, the faster one tends to walk and so the earlier one can arrive at an albergue – ipso facto one is allocated a bottom bunk; the older one is, the slower one walks and one inevitably ends up on the top bunk!

We were grateful for the beds, but worried that the Korean mother and daughter below us would wake up every time we rolled over, leave alone when we had to get up in the night. We showered and did laundry. There was one shower and one toilet for each gender!! We would not have designed a hostel like that. Ayn and Michael from California were also staying at this hostel and we leant them one of our stretchy washing lines, although the sudden down pour of rain meant we all had to rush to get the laundry in before it was fully dry. We were finding that our underwear and light-weight tops tended to dry overnight in the warmth generated by so many bodies in the same room. Dinner was very substantial and very delicious. There was a pay-computer at the albergue so we were able to update our blog, something we were enjoying doing as with no books, apart from our guide book, there was little else to do in the evening.

Blog (Charlotte) Monday, 6 May 2013 Tilting at windmills: day Five.

Charlotte: we are showered and changed and feeling tired but we have had a lovely day walking in the sun. We had stayed in a lovely hotel in Pamplona and were spoilt with our own bathroom. I am realising how important these things are to me. We started out at 07:45 out through the suburbs of Pamplona which is a beautiful city, very green with many mature trees and green spaces, all kept neat and tidy. It is always harder to walk on pavement but we soon headed along a track, steadily climbing to Alto del Perdon the highest point today and for many days to come. We stopped many times to rest and drink loads of water. Jane's plan to take things gently at first is working well, though weary at the end of the day I am not exhausted. There was quite a throng of pilgrims on the route today. If this is the quiet season it must be crazy come the summer. Now I must thank Mark my brother, as I have become a convert - thank you Mark for leaving behind some of your big hankies when you have stayed at my house as I have snaffled them and they are totally useful. I shall return them, laundered of course, when I return

I am missing my family and friends especially my darling boy, Arlen. Do please keep me and Jane in your thoughts and keep in touch, love to you all.

Jane: It was like walking in a very warm British summer today. You understand why there is a tradition of pilgrims getting out as early as they can. You want to avoid a lot of the heat and, of course you may have to walk much further on to find your bed for the night if you get in too late to the village you've targeted. Highlights of the day today were: beautiful aromas as we passed loads of spring flowers and bushes in full bloom, a lovely yellow-breasted bird singing its heart out on a low bush, the splendid (if hazy) view from on top of Alto del Perdon where a huge wind farm competes with a metal art installation of groups of pilgrims leaning into the wind. (Older people will understand the title of the blog now).

We amazed ourselves that night by having the best sleep of the pilgrimage so far. We cannot comment on how it was for the ladies below us.

Day 6. May 7th Uterga – Lorca   20.2K/12.6M   (stayed in Albergue La Bodega del Camino)

We were awake early and out walking by 07.15. We fuelled ourselves with a drink of water and an energy bar before setting off as there was no bar open yet. The air smelt heavenly – cool and fresh but it quickly warmed up. This was a day of rolling ups and downs – ultimately very tiring. If we could characterise this day it would be by scent and perfume. We were overwhelmed by the heady mix of the perfume of herbs, wild flowers and blossoms. We had a long stop after a couple of hours of walking at Puente la Reina where we had two coffees and some cake. We stopped first at one hotel/café where pilgrims were still having breakfast and their suitcases were being loaded onto vans for onward transit. We then went to a bakery café where we bumped into Luca, the young Italian from the hostel in Roncesvalles. We were surprised to meet him as we had assumed he would be miles ahead. However, he had had a bad fall coming down from the Alto del Perdon, damaging his hip badly and had been resting up before continuing. The doctor he had seen had advised he should return home to Sicily. He appeared to be pleased to see us, speak a little Italian and have someone care about his injuries. We were not to see him again so we hope he made it to Santiago.

We visited a farmacia, the first of many occasions, to get something for Jane's upset stomach. We realised that for the Spanish these transactions had to be treated as mini social occasions with much chat and gossip – a very good thing, especially for the elderly who might have more need of social engagement than the average member of the working population. What it did do for us was to create another opportunity to practice our developing patience.

Eventually we left the busy little town of Puente la Reina and began the long plod up to the hill top village of Maneru. We hoped to stop once we had got to the top, but once there we found no obvious place to rest or bar to visit. This disappointment was completely forgotten when we came across the most unbelievably exciting zoological find. Resting on the paving stones in a small public square surrounded by a few trees was the largest butterfly we had ever seen outside of a zoo. Research by Charlotte's grandson's other granny revealed later that it was not a butterfly, but instead was the largest European moth. It was beautiful and very big.

The Saturnia Pyri seen at Maneru on the way to Lorca on May 7ᵗʰ (day 6)

With much reluctance we had to leave our lepidopteran discovery, having placed the moth safely beneath a tree rather on the main pilgrim path. Almost immediately, as we left the village Jane saw on the verge a huge, emerald green lizard – what was it with this hilltop village that all its creatures were so big?

Perhaps because we were excited by the things we had seen that day, perhaps because we were too busy chatting, perhaps because we were getting blasé about finding our way along the route, we ended up getting lost! One minute we were walking along some genuine old Roman cobbles, the next we are emerging onto a complex, very modern motorway and roundabout interconnection – with no yellow arrows to be seen anywhere. Risking life and limb we galumphed across the multi-lane interconnection (well you try running with a huge pack on your back and you'll find you galumph too) when we were hailed by a Korean cyclist who had been resting on the grass of the roundabout. He pointed us in a general direction and with some anxiety we headed off that way. The Camino cyclists in part follow the walkers' route, but they also diverge on occasions; we hoped we were not setting off on a busy road diversion. It was with much relief after about half a mile that we picked up the Camino way marks again and we could see where we should have walked through a subway under the motor way. This taught us a lesson; we had to stay a little more alert!

On arrival at Lorca we were delighted to meet a welcoming receptionist and we decided to get a room with its own loo. After a lovely shower and the usual laundry we went down to have a much needed drink. Here we met a charming young Spanish man, Diego, who was nursing an inflamed knee. He was doing a section of the Way, meeting his wife in Burgos and was hoping the icepack on his knee would reduce the inflammation enough for him to continue. As with Luca, the descent from the Alto del Perdon had caused his injury; the slow-and-steady approach of the older woman can clearly be recommended over the rush and dash of the younger man! We were hoping to stop at Villamayor de Monjardin the following day and Diego kindly volunteered to book us in saying it was perfectly possible to do this. Unfortunately when he got through to the hostel he was told that it was not permitted to book ahead, which is what we had assumed from all the discussions on the Forum that we had read before we left home.

We shared our supper table with two French men, Jean-Jacques and Alain, who were walking the Way in memory of a deceased child in Alain's family – Jane could not quite grasp whose child it was and did not like to ask too many prying questions. It was a good work-out for the language skills, but a little exhausting. After supper we wandered around the tiny village of Lorca and saw for the first time the evidence of the numerous swifts, swallow and martins that would delight us in the days to come; there were whole cities of martins' nests under the eaves of the local houses. Ayn and Michael were staying in the albergue opposite ours and had found it a little chaotic so Ayn had voluntarily swept the bar floor for the proprietor whilst waiting for supper to be cooked. We sat outside chatting in the evening, but it became too chilly so we went to bed early once more.

Day 7. May 8th Lorca – Villamayor de Monjardin   18K/11.3M (stayed at Dutch albergue Hogar Monjardin)

We started walking early at 06.55 after a good night. There was a gentle mizzling rain in the air which meant we got too warm with our wet-weather gear on. It was another rolling path day with many undulations all culminating in a biggish climb to get to our day's destination – a Christian volunteer hostel. We were both tired today with aching backs and to boost energy we would treat ourselves to one of the "midget gem" sweeties Jane had brought from home. The rain ceased fairly quickly and the day was pleasant but overcast. The sights we saw, by contrast, were far from dull. We were becoming aware that Spain is full of bridges, ancient and modern, grand and rustic. This day we walked over a steep, modern slatted bridge that looked like a piece of artwork.

We were shortly entranced by a fearsome sculptural relief above the door of a church, the Iglesia Parroquial del Santo Sepulcro. It would have been very clear to the humble folk in pre-literacy days that the damned would come to a sticky end -- they were destined to be swallowed by a satanic monster – it would certainly terrify you into remembering your Ps and Qs and keeping your eyes off your neighbour's ass! The scaremongering would have been important as the contrasting depiction of where the blessed souls went was a little mundane – you'd get a halo if you are good. What amazed us was not just this graphic encouragement to the souls of the parish, but the fact that it remained in such good condition, although the figures in the Last Supper relief below were far more worn away. Of course, the church itself was closed, as all churches in Spain appeared to be. After a short climb we came to the Bodegas Irache which was a winery behind which was a fountain dispensing free red wine to anyone who wanted some. Charlotte had a taste – from her scallop shell for authenticity; Jane just had water. In the space of a short morning we moved from heavenly contemplation to earthly pleasures.

One of the urban delights we had been noticing was a type of tree with a bluish grey peeling bark. These trees had their main branches cut and trained to bump into each other so that over time the branches of the trees grew together forming a lattice work of branches criss-crossing above your head. All the minor branches were then pollarded so that in summer the new growth would form a ceiling of leaves to protect people below from the sun – it was ingenious. The trees (perhaps a species of lime tree) were clearly fast growing as one we saw had almost consumed an attached notice with enveloping bark.

As we walked that day we saw far away to our right the distant sight of mountains. Towards mid-day Ayn and Michael caught up with us. They were faster walkers than us two but had left later. We walked (quite swiftly) together for the rest of the morning until we arrived at Villamayor de Monjardin at 13.00. We were allocated a room together but could not formally register until 16.00. This albergue was run by a Dutch Christian group who staffed the hostel with volunteers who came for a couple of months or a couple of weeks as they could. It was an ancient place, all steep stone steps, odd-angled and beamed rooms and one shower/toilet room for everyone. The weather was overcast but Charlotte risked doing some laundry. Having had our showers and done our chores we became aware of an altercation at the entrance to the hostel. The slightly quirky French lady we had met in Zubiri was trying to persuade the hostpitalero that there must be room for one old lady walking on her own. Unfortunately there was no room left; the hostel had already put additional sleeping mats down in the lobby and could only offer, an outside shelter or the bus or they could phone for a taxi for her. We realised that we were very lucky to get in. There were a good number of people waiting at the bus stop and others were calling for taxis. The taxi drivers were saying that the next village was full as well. Jane's developing anxiety about finding beds for the night was now becoming acute. We went into the little square to find a drink and snack and posted a short blog without any attached photos. There was a group of young pilgrims enjoying each other's company and numerous glasses of beer; they remained there the whole afternoon. Here we met up with Susie and Cecilia, the intrepid 70 year olds who had started out in Le Puy in France. Cecilia was very engaged on the phone clearly booking accommodation for the following day. When Jane asked her how she was able to do this, she explained that so long as the albergue was private, one could book ahead. Bed problem solved – or so we thought.

After a communal supper many of the pilgrims went for a Christian meditation session whilst we went for a wander around the tiny, hilly village. We would have been happy to attend a meditative period of reflection, but it was "sold" as a "Jesus meditation" which we found a little off-putting. The day had been mild but the evening was chilly and we were both glad of our cosy sleeping bags that night. On one dark trip down to the toilets that night Charlotte discovered one of the youngsters who had been drinking in the square all afternoon in a very sorry state. He had clearly been very sick and was recovering and sipping water and was also very embarrassed – there are many ways to approach a pilgrimage! We woke very early and decided we would try and quietly leave. We had read about the noisy early-departers who disturb other people's rest flashing their torches around and packing their rucksacks noisily. We avoided putting on our torches to minimise the disturbance to Ayn and Michael and tried desperately to remember where we had placed everything the previous evening. One of the tests we had had to pass, donkeys' years before when we had been girl guides, was to wrap up a camping bedding roll in a waterproof groundsheet in the dark and tie all the correct knots to hold it in place. One just never knows when such skills are going to come in handy again! We got out of the room with most of our stuff in our hands, not in the rucksacks; perhaps we had not remembered all our packing bedding roll skills after all. The next challenge was to retrieve our boots from the boot rack behind the two pilgrims sleeping on the floor mats in the lobby area – it was kind of inevitable that we would disturb them. Outside in the fresh morning cool we had to pack everything from scratch and get our boots on.

We did this together with a German husband and wife who were also creeping out very early. We would keep meeting this couple for some time and then suddenly no more. We were off walking with head torch on at 06.25.

Blog (Jane) Wednesday, 8 May 2013 The Big and The Little

Yesterday and today (Tuesday & Wednesday) we have been walking through pretty, rolling countryside; lots of hills, rivers, bridges, hilltop villages. Yes, OK there have been the occasional cement factory and vast brewery and the odd ugly town -- but mostly lovely. We are both tired now and will rest up in Logrono for two nights to give ourselves a treat.

We have decided to count the "angels" we meet on the way. Our first "angel" was a young French man we met at Biarritz who took pity on us patiently waiting for the bus into Bayonne and came and told us that as it was 1st May there were no buses. He then gave us his place in the long taxi queue. Our second "angel" was a lovely American women who took pity on Charlotte when she wanted to change her bunk bed allocation from one bay (which happened to be full of a group of friends) to my bay, which was empty. She rescued Charlotte from a very severe Mrs Jobsworth and was later very solicitous of our wellbeing and remembered our names. Our third was a Korean cyclists who saw us in the distance, hailed us (appreciating we had missed the path) and pointed us in the right direction.

Amazing things we have seen recently: an emerald green lizard as long and fat as a small kitten -- OK there is no picture to prove this, but enter the "spirit of the Camino" and believe me; the biggest, most spectacular moth we have ever seen outside of a zoo (please, Mary, if you can, tell us what it is) -- just tried to load picture but no can do this time. Wait with baited breath as it is truly stunning and you wouldn't want a couple of them batting around your lampshade.

Day 8. May 9th Villamayor de Monjardin – Torres del Rio 19.5K/12.2M (stayed at La Pata de Oca albergue)

We set off at a brisk pace a little worried that we might have left things behind in our anxiety not to make too much noise when we left the albergue in the dark. We had not been able to apply our usual anti-inflammatory gel because of leaving in the dark so we had to stop to do this as both of us were finding our backs very achy that day. Walking was easy along gravelled tracks beside farmers' fields and through wooded areas. The dominant sensation was of perfumes as we passed an abundance of varied wild flowers in the hedgerows and glorious pink, purple and mauve tamarisk trees. After seven miles we stopped for a much needed café con leche and doughnut at Los Arcos. It was now very overcast and whilst not cold, fine drizzly rain was settling in. We got into a stride after this but chose not to put on wet weather gear which might have been a mistake if the distance to our destination had been longer. We were drenched through by the time we arrived at Torres del Rio after a steep climb down and then up to the village. There was room at the inn, La Pata de Oca and the hostpitalero insisted on carrying our two heavy packs up to our room. We were the first in the room he allocated us so we chose the two bottom bunks – very snug – we could not sit up or even perch on the edge – there can be merits to being on the top bunk. There were plentiful showers and toilets and we draped our wet things around to dry.

We went out to explore the little village – everything was closed, including the celebrated church. We returned to the albergue to warm up, but with all the doors open for the comings and goings of pilgrims it was cold here too. In our room we met Claude, a French lady a little older than us. Claude was walking by herself, her companion having given up very early on. Claude had no English so Jane's French was truly put to the test, but probably only scored 5/10 in that exam. Claude had already walked the Camino Way a number of years before and was going to take the train from Burgos to Sarria on this occasion and meet up with her companion there. Whilst our rucksack straps were soaking from the continuous drizzle, Claude's were bone dry as she had worn a long poncho enclosing both her and her sack. We were just beginning to see there could be some merits in these pilgrim ponchos. We put on our warmest walking socks and went to have a reviving coffee. We met up with the German couple from that morning and Ayn and Michael, who were staying elsewhere but using the laundry and restaurant facilities at this albergue.

We had been very impressed with this albergue (despite its being a bit cold) but then we had the pilgrim's menu meal. This was a bizarre affair. Claude sat with us and the three of us all ordered slightly different dishes from the menu. This was a mistake. People were served by dish rather than by table. Anyone having salad got served first, then when they had finished people starting with pasta got served and the salad people got their main course. Meanwhile the bean starter people sat and waited. The pasta people now got their main course whilst by now the salad people had eaten everything except a desert and the bean people were still waiting. Any prompting of the waitress brought a torrent of confused, rather cross explanation. The waitress passing by to another table paused briefly to throw a choc ice at Jane and Claude – Charlotte had not yet had a bite to eat! The bean dish, when it finally arrived was very tasty. By the time Charlotte had her choc ice chucked at her, the rest of us at the table had long since finished – not the most companionable of communal meals! At this point we heard a familiar voice; in the corner, just starting his meal (we hoped he had not ordered beans) was Canadian Bill – hugs all round. We never saw him again, but we wished him well.

Despite the strange service at the evening meal we decided to have coffee and toast before leaving in the morning so we had a far more leisurely start than the previous day and were not walking until 8.05am.

Walking out next morning

Blog (Jane) Thursday, 9 May 2013 Crack of Dawn

Well we surprised even ourselves by getting up at 05.45 and starting today's walk at 06.25. It was a bit of a challenge getting out of the room we were sharing with a couple of Americans without starting an international incident. Do you just go for it irrespective of noise and get those backpacks stuffed, or do you tippy-toe around trying to make as little noise as possible? The compromise we ended up with meant we had to completely re-pack the bags outside the albergue as mine was so badly packed. We also had to extract our boots from behind where two pilgrims were sleeping on mattresses on the floor in front of the boot rack. Apparently walking the Camino Way in May is "the new black" so albergues are getting filled up fairly early in the afternoon. Many people had to get buses or taxis to a point further along the route as the village we were in and the next one along were both full by 4.00pm. Anyway we arrived here, Torres del Rio at 12.35 and we have a BOTTOM BUNK and there are 3 loos!! What more could you want?!

The morning's walk was lovely, through Spanish farmland and passing amazing hedgerow flowers - such variety and colour and scents. It was fresh - which is nice for walking, but it was over 8 kilometres to our first coffee, so that was a bit of a stretch. It was a cloudy day and we ended walking for hour and half in the rain; better tomorrow I believe.

Blog (Charlotte): Everything Jane has described I could have written. I felt weary today but chuffed to be on our way so early. We got to hear the dawn chorus and the air was scented with perfume from the hedgerow plants. We came across tamarisk trees in full flower, pink all over with a pungent perfume which filled the air. I wish you could see the amazing variety of spring flowers growing wild that we have to buy from garden centres. I am still coughing but I do feel my chest is getting better. It is lovely to get to the albergue each day, shower and change and then rest before the evening meal. Bedtime is getting earlier and earlier. Thank you all of you for your comments; they made us laugh and mean so much to us. We are going to raise a glass tonight to our first full week on the Camino. We are now in Rioja having walked through Navarre; many miles to go but we face each day as it comes.

First seven days in five words:

Charlotte´s:	**Jane´s:**
Surprising, Challenging, Scented, Extraordinary, Doable	Discombobulating, Sensual, Challenging, Sociable, Foreign

Blog (Jane) Please keep this to yourselves, but I do try to keep Charlotte off the old vino; any opportunity she can get! Whereas, in contrast, I merely had water. (This was the fuente del vino, a free red wine fountain at Bodegas Irache)

Now do you believe us! When we said huge, we meant huge!

After these first eight days we were very slowly beginning to feel our way into the pilgrim life. Whilst we were still not sleeping very well, we were getting used to the protocols of shared hostel living. We were getting used to the daily walking with large packs, although we ached and were very tired. We were enjoying the countryside and we enjoyed bumping into people we had already met. It still felt as if there was a huge distance to go (there was) and we were very daunted, but we were fractionally less disturbed by the strangeness than we had been – we were beginning to "bed down".

Journal reflection (Jane): I am not feeling remotely inclined to be reflective as I walk along. Most of the time when I am walking I am simply gawping about me taking in the scenery, talking to Charlotte or chatting to other pilgrims as we meet up and walk together for a while. We also stop to take photos, to look at a particularly beautiful bank of poppies or an unusual wild flower, to agree which branch of the path to take or to decide where to stop for a break – it is all largely practical stuff. Inevitably there are many opportunities to people watch. One of the things I am trying not to get exercised over is the way most walkers mis-use their walking poles. I am not only a convert to walking poles for the additional support they give and the damage they prevent to hips and knees, but I am also a convert to their correct usage. When Henry and I had done the Coast to Coast long distance walk back in the UK we had met an American, Geoff, and walked with him for a couple of days. One day he asked me if I had ever been taught how to use my poles. Well, I thought he was mad – like asking if I had been taught to use my boots or my cagoule. As it transpired he had gone on a course when he bought his poles (the things they offer in America!) Geoff showed me how one should use the pole on the opposite side to the forward moving leg and not swing the poles hugely and randomly around. It took a little practice, but was incredibly effective – and screamingly obvious once pointed out. Anyway, now on the Camino Way I have to overcome the temptation a dozen times a day to stop pilgrims and put them right about how to use their poles. I have to keep telling myself to let it go, to not get irritated by people. It is not a very profound reflection, but that is as deep as it gets at the moment.

I am still feeling enormously homesick and missing Henry – it is strange how I can have the two contradictory emotions simultaneously: wanting to be back at home and wanting to crack on with the pilgrimage.

Journal reflection (Charlotte): One week down and I am getting used to the routine. I am looking forward to a rest at Logroño and feel very comfortable about combining the "soft and the hard" in order to manage this adventure of the Way. I think we are managing very well given we were neither of us in tip-top condition before we began.

CHAPTER SIX   ON AND OFF THE WAY

Day 9. May 10th   Torres del Rio – Logroño –20.6K/12.9M (stayed at AC Hotel La Rioja)

Day nine started off very cold and ended up very warm. We were both looking forward to our first rest day. Originally we had thought we would not have a rest day until we reached Burgos. However, because of our health problems the first part of the pilgrimage had been more exhausting than we had anticipated so we added in this extra stop. Henry had booked us a place to stay for two nights but with much difficulty (pilgrims are not allowed to stay in municipal albergues for more than one night without a medical reason to). He texted to say that all the central places he first tried were fully booked so he had to go for somewhere a little away from the centre.

The walk from Torres del Rio to Viana was cold but pleasant, walking alongside farmers' fields on gravel tracks. When we got to Viana we were delighted to find a hikers shop which was open. Not only was it open, but when we entered we found we could purchase rubber bungs for the ends of our walking poles. This might appear to be a strange thing to get excited about, but these "anti-click-clacks" were going to prove a godsend. We immediately put them on and could now walk through this town using our poles with no disturbance to the good citizens of Spain. These little additions to our kit would prove to be worth their weight in gold in terms of saving our backs and preserving our energy in the weeks ahead. On no other occasion were we to come across a hikers shop in such a serendipitous manner. We sat in an ugly little square on the outskirts of this slightly grim town to eat our lunch before the final walk down into Logroño. This part of the walk was through many ugly suburbs, past industrial sites and waste and scrub land. As we approached Logroño the sun came out and it immediately became very warm. We stopped to get our credencials stamped by an old lady, Felisa, as we moved into the region of Rioja. Her aunt had set this stall up, selling badges and stamping credencials for a donation and the niece continues the tradition.

We turned left after crossing the huge Puente de Piedra over the river Ebro whereas the Camino Way continued in the other direction. We had to find our hotel for the next two nights. We plodded and plodded, the area not looking particularly salubrious. In the far distance we could see a grey concrete multi-story car park but nothing that looked like a hotel. We asked directions but no one was sure. We arrived at the multi-story car park and realised it was an office block – but no – once we had walked past it we saw a door round the side hidden by pillars with a modest sign declaring it was the hotel we were looking for – talk about hiding one's light under a bushel!

Once more we met the strange Spanish reception manner – ignore the guest, there are better things to do. After some considerable time the young lady, who was immediately under our noses, left her computer and served us – she could have done with taking some lessons from her Pamplona counterpart! Our room was fine, but we needed our universal bath plug for the bath. Bathing and laundry completed we were too tired to walk into town so decided to eat at the hotel but have a drink first as there was a bar. Well, there was a bar but no bar staff, so back to the reluctant receptionist and after much telephoning she found somebody to serve us a drink – it was worth the wait as we were introduced to hotel measure gin and tonics. We were presented with a tray full of different types of gin and a glass goblet the size of a small goldfish bowl full of ice. Charlotte chose a gin and the bar woman just poured it over the ice; we had no idea whether we were supposed to say "when" but eventually we gestured it was enough. We had a gin and tonic big enough to satisfy at least four keen gin drinkers, a huge bowl of nuts and another of olives – we both dreaded the bill – but we enjoyed the G and T! We had to wait some time to eat as Spanish people eat their evening meal at around 9.00pm or later. We were quite sloshed by the time we got to the rather empty hotel restaurant, but the food was nice. Jane went to bed with a migraine and drugs but we were both looking forward to exploring the city the following day.

Our hotel in Logroño

Day 10. Rest Day May 11th

This was such a strange day. Neither of us was expecting to feel so out of sorts with ordinary big town living. It started off badly as we could not get the expensive, pay-card non-wireless computer in the hotel lobby to work and we had been really looking forward to updating the blog and uploading some photos. Family and friends were also beginning to leave comments and we found these messages from home so comforting that to forego them was upsetting. We had rather assumed a hotel would have had up-to-date IT facilities, but perhaps people now all carry their own tablets and laptops. We walked into the town along broad non-descript roads but had great difficulty with the bank APR machines. We both needed to get more money out but the first attempt failed for both of us as did the next machine. At the third Jane was able to get money out but Charlotte could not. It is strange how something that would be simply annoying at home becomes worrying and distressing when abroad. We depended on these machines working for us as we were not carrying large sums of money in cash. As it transpired we had not done our translation of sterling into euros correctly and we were asking for sums just fractionally over our withdrawal limits – no problemo – except it was a problemo at the time. Charlotte later called the emergency number she had been given by her bank only to get a recorded voice and began to feel rather panicked and tearful – an emotion precipitated as much by the strangeness of our adventure as by the conundrum of how to get money to support our travels. Our next problem was that we could not find any bread for the following day's picnic lunch; what we could find was too stale or too seedy or too big or too small. In actuality we were again just failing to deal with the normal complexities of daily choices that we did not have to deal with when living the simple life of a pilgrim on the Way. We had a little more success in choosing postcards to send to our grandchildren and in finding somewhere to have a light lunch. We drank coffee in a square and watched the many hen and stag groups that were congregating. The things we enjoyed most about Logrono was the statue of the pilgrims – a reminder of who were really were – and the huge bags of live snails available for purchase at a vegetable shop – a reminder that we were in a different country should we need that reminder.

We were glad to return to our strange hotel where a huge children's party was running amok everywhere fuelled by enormous bags of sweets. We were also pleased to discover a different receptionist on duty who kindly agreed to book two beds for us at a private hostel in Ventosa, our destination for the following day. Once more we ate in the hotel as there was no way would we venture into the town again and we chilled in our room trying to fathom the Spanish weather forecasts on the TV. We were looking forward to being back on the simple path of the pilgrim the following day.

Day 11. May 12th Logroño – Ventosa 19.7K/12.3M (stayed at San Saturnino albergue)

Logroño's parting gift to us the morning of our departure was horrid. We set out at 07.05, the only people around apart from some cruising

86

police cars. For the first time it felt a little eerie. We regained the Camino Way path and picked up the signs and began walking through the deserted city centre. Then from nowhere came a loud, aggressive and very drunk Spanish man. He stood in front of us and, despite our lack of Spanish, it was clear to us he was aggressively swearing and threatening us. As we stepped around him and picked up speed so did he, chasing us and continuing to shout and swear and leap in front of us. There was no one else around. Where were all the other early morning pilgrims? Where were those cruising police cars? This continued for some time with both of us refusing to engage with him but marching along as briskly as we could. Eventually, as we neared the edge of the town centre he gave up, bellowing more abuse at us. We had not enjoyed Logroño the previous day and we certainly felt no sadness to be leaving that morning. We were so rattled by this unexpected assault on us that we maintained our ludicrously swift pace for the next six kilometres until we came to a delightful park with an open café. We were exhausted already. Charlotte wondered whether what had triggered this drunken man's fury at us was Jane's Tilley sun hat – did he think it was an American cowboy hat and that we were Americans? – She thought she caught something about Americans in what he was saying. Well, bang went all our charitable feelings to our fellow mankind – our rest stop in Logroño had set us backwards on a number of levels.

We tried to find our equilibrium again over a coffee and doughnut then walked on to the pretty little town of Navarette. We sat for ages outside the Church of the Assumption before realising it was open and we could go in. Now this was an unexpected event as we had found until this day that the vast majority of Spanish churches are kept locked up, presumably for security reasons and because the parish priests have to each serve a very wide area. We went in. We could not see a thing as it was pitch dark. We groped our way to where votive candles were available to purchase and light. Charlotte had promised a friend she would light candles on the Way for his departed partner. Once the candle was lit we could begin to make out a truly splendid and enormous gold altar piece rising up behind the altar – no wonder they have to keep the churches locked if this amount of precious metal adorned all the churches. Spiritual duties done, we went down to a café for a coffee and heard our first English voice since leaving home – Brian from Liverpool.

This meeting with Brian from Liverpool was an example of how on the Camino Way one can meet someone for a fleetingly short period and yet speak to them about important things and be lifted by their concern. Brian was probably in his thirties and had been in the army and following that had taught self-defence classes. He had started with an army friend who had been wounded whilst on service. The friend had returned home as his injuries prevented his continuing. On hearing of our horrid encounter that morning he gave us some practical advice on how to cope in similar situations. One piece of advice was to find the most disgustingly obscenely rude thing we could think of and scream it as loudly as we could. He said it was surprising how quickly the sound of women being foul-mouthed attracted attention. Brian was walking with a German, Tomas, who had recently befriended him and helped him find better walking boots that fitted. We spoke for perhaps 10 to 15 minutes before they left the bar, but we both felt better for our meeting with them. Suddenly behind us we heard, "It's the British ladies!", and there was Bethany whom last we had seen leaving Roncesvalles having lost her walking poles and having sent her pack on as it was too heavy. She now had another set of poles and her rucksack and a walking companion, Jenny from Germany. It was lovely to see her again, but we were about to leave and they were both about to start their lunch.

It was just under five miles to Ventosa and we arrived there at 14.30. The hostel owner asked us to not only leave our boots in the hall, but to also leave our poles. They had recently had an "incident" where a pilgrim had complained of being woken in the night by being jabbed in the stomach by a walking pole to stop him snoring. It must have been some jab to cause a complaint! When shown to our room we fell over backwards to discover Bethany and Jenny already there – how had they managed that; there was only one route to Ventosa and we had not seen them pass us?

There were twelve people in each room and about four rooms, good shower/toilet facilities, a kitchen and a pretty little garden that acted as a sun trap. We both managed to get a bottom bunk, but then two young German men, both Scouts arrived: one long tall bean pole, the other a complete opposite, in girth at least. The beanpole went above Charlotte and the large lad above Jane. The bunks here were of a very broad and sturdy design – just as well. By now the entire room, with the exception of Bethany and us two, was German. When this dominance by one nationality happens it can be a bit exclusive. We sat in the garden to get warm as earlier we had got very cold, possibly partly a result of the shock of our morning encounter. Here we met a Dutch physicist, Giese (pronounced "geese") who later ate with us in the village. His wife was a professional singer and would be joining him later when her engagements allowed. All the German youngsters also congregated in the garden to play card games and eat sandwiches. We were to see this group of young people all the way from here to just short of Leon. We wondered why they did shortish days for unlike us, it seemed they could have walked further. We later learnt that several were on breaks before starting University or new jobs and had time to kill. The day had started badly but ended very pleasantly.

We set off early the next morning having slept reasonably well and were walking by 07.30 beneath a clear blue sky but with a cold breeze accompanying us.

Journal reflection (Charlotte): F......, stinking men! Sometimes they are so vile! The drunk b...... who had a go at us as we were leaving Logroño was foul. Poor Jane – he directed his anger at Jane first and then at both of us. I have let it go. I know there are so many loving and gently men in my life, but it always hurts when patriarchy and misogyny hits you in the face and guts. Glad to leave Logroño – never to return! After meeting Brian from Liverpool and Tomas from Germany in Navarrete, my heart felt lighter and I felt more like a pilgrim again – faith restored. Once at Ventosa, relaxing in the garden of the albergue I felt physically and mentally more relaxed than I have done for days.

Dear Reader, as you can see from this journal entry written at the time, we had been very disturbed by the attack on us in Logroño, but equally, other pilgrims had helped restore our faith in humanity.

Day 12. May 13th Ventosa – Azofra 16.2K/10.1M (stayed at municipal albergue)

We passed many rural vineyards that day. The vines are all free-standing and not trained onto wires as one sees in France and Italy. The vines had all been pruned low to the ground and were just beginning to sprout a few new green leaves. The trunks were old, gnarly and contorted. Presumably this form of cultivation suited this species of grape. This day was a day of splendid vistas with distant mountains in almost all directions.

Views of distant mountains

Beautiful scenery is a joy to the soul; it uplifts you without you even realising it. As we set off there was mist in the valleys and we strode out on wide dry tracks. The red Rioja earth is supposed to become claggily sticky after rain, but fortunately it was dry that day. We had no need to rush as we were only intending to walk around ten miles so we stopped at Najera for a couple of coffees and met up with Bethany and Jenny.

We arrived at the municipal albergue in Azofra at 12.30, amongst the first to arrive. We were allocated a cubicle with two beds, shelves for our packs and swing doors – a bit like a high cowboy-type saloon door. There were unisex showers and toilets, a large kitchen and communal area and a large outdoor sitting area including a little foot pool. It was a glorious afternoon so we did loads of laundry and got it outside to dry. We had the whole afternoon to relax and wander around. The village was small and took little time to explore. The most fascinating sight for us was the statue of the Virgin Mary dedicated to Rioja. Of itself this was not especially noteworthy; there are many statues of the Virgin Mary throughout the area of Spain we had walked through. This one however, was unusual: she sat behind glass with the Baby Jesus on her lap – so far, so good. Without wanting to cause offense and without wanting to be inappropriately blasphemous, we could not but help see that the sculptor of the Baby had created him to look exactly like a ventriloquist's dummy. In addition, the sculptor had given the Baby the most enormous feet and, to top it all he had put the feet on back to front! We just fell about; it was the funniest thing we had seen for a long time. We could not fathom this very odd statue; was the extraordinary depiction of the Christ Child significant in some way or was this simply the product of a surfeit of the local Rioja after which the statue was dedicated? An extremely jovial and pleasant ancient local man approached us, clearly very pleased to see our admiration of their prized Virgin – fortunately he had no English.

After our tour of the village we discovered that all the Germans from

Ventosa had arrived at the hostel as well as Bethany and Jenny. They were all chilling in the outdoor area, one of the lads lounging in the hammock he was carrying with him – well it takes all sorts – some people cut the labels off their clothes to make their packs lighter and would probably resist the temptation to carry a hammock! Another group of young men were avidly discussing the attractiveness of some girls they had met; one of this group was a young American doctor (Americans can have very carrying voices, so one hears all sorts). It was this young man that Charlotte burst in on in the showers as he had not locked the door – she did not comment on his attractions or otherwise, politely saying she had not got her specs on at the time! We had not been able to update our blog now for a number of days so we spent some time and euros reassuring everyone all was well with us – we did not mention the Logrono incident as there was no point in worrying anyone.

Blog (Jane) Monday, 13 May 2013 Better Late than Never

Hi everyone! So sorry that there has been a deafening silence, but technology has either let us down or we have been so remote there has been no technology. We thought we'd tell you all a little about life as a modern-day pilgrim, if we can put it into words. We are very slowly settling into this itinerant life. We quite like the communal albergues, but it is nice when you get little "bays" or rooms for two, as we have today. Sometimes you can chat to other pilgrims and hear of their experiences and you end up sharing loads with total strangers most of whom you never see again. Sometimes, however, one nationality dominates and it can then be a little exclusive. Sometimes you meet pilgrims who you would think would be friendly (eg a bunch of Irish) who can be dismissively unpleasant. On the whole the pilgrim community is friendly and mutually helpful. When we step off The Way for a much needed rest, it is completely confusing. We felt very alienated for our rest day in Logroño (we would say cancel your planned holiday there; Pamplona is far nicer). Just walking every day, in quite cool weather that becomes sunnier as we move into the afternoon, is very liberating. The only worries are: will we get a bed where we plan to stop, can we find a shop open to buy provisions, and where on earth is the next loo!

Blog (Charlotte): On the theme of what it feels like to be a pilgrim, Katherine gave her Mum some sound advice which was to be prepared to feel quite strange for at least two weeks if not more, how true her words have proved to be for both of us. Today we walked from Ventosa to Azofra, the sky was blue, sun shining but a cool breeze blew. The soil is rose red and the landscape full of vines and cereal crops, apart from the occasional farm worker and mangy dog the only other people were pilgrims and few of them today. It was beautiful, bird song, flowers and the gentle but steady pace and the sound of our sticks. That is what we have come to feel as the true pilgrim day. It was a shock to me how Logroño knocked me off kilter. We needed the rest and it did us a huge amount of good but we are already planning how to cope with the change from walking the way to resting. Good learning experience and hard to convey as this is such a unique experience for me. As all who know me know I am not a 'believer' but special things do happen on this strange path, brief intense contacts, small favours offered and pleasure in swift friendships. Yesterday, feeling out of sorts and a bit fragile I heard an English voice, Brian from Liverpool traveling with Tomas from Germany; we spoke for less than 15 minutes but it buoyed us up for the rest of the day. He was so kind and he himself described how Tomas had befriended him at a low point and were now travelling together.

Navarette, the Church was open here (!!)

Blog (Jane) Monday, 13 May 2013 Some Funny Things We´ve Seen

As we have walked along we have been taking snaps of this and that and we realised we have seen many rather unusual or odd things. We thought we would share a few with you.

The land is so lush and the plants so potent, they have to be corralled in cages.

Walking The Way can be a very "other-worldly" experience. The other world crept up on me recently as I was walking when Darth Vader appeared over my shoulder!

I thought we were all walking rather slowly, but it suited the mood I was in.

If pilgrims are too weary to move fast the Munchy Tree will get them!

95

We wouldn't dare wave a red rag at this bull.

Less than two weeks walking and I'm changing my walking companion.

After a pilgrim's menu supper at the bar in the village and after updating the blog, once more we were to bed early. We both slept only moderately well and there was the inevitable need to get up in the dark and creep down the corridor to the washroom area. It was on one such occasion that Jane had a bit of a scare. It is possible that she was pre-disposed to be shocked as a result of the Logrono incident, or just being sleepy was not thinking straight. Jane was returning from her second visit to the loos, tip-toeing back along the gloomy corridor and creeping into her bed bay so as not to disturb Charlotte. She fumbled around at the top of her bed to try and identify the opening of her sleeping bag and was utterly surprised to discover someone had climbed into her bed! What to do? Scream, try and find the lights, shout? As the interloper began to murmur and wake up, Jane beat a hasty retreat, heart thumping and frantically asking herself what on earth was going on? Outside the door the small room number indicated bay six, which did not make sense as it should have said seven. As quick as lightening Jane scooted into bay seven realising her error, climbed into her (empty) sleeping bag and convulsed with laughter. We had no idea who was in bay six, but the next morning we realised the occupants were two of the German boys. We decided not to reveal that it was one of the English grannies who had tried to climb into bed with them. We thought it kinder to leave them to whatever their fantasy might have been.

Day 13. May 14th Azofra – Granon   22.4K/14M (stayed at Church run donativo albergue at Granon)

We were up at 06.00 and walking at 07.15. We wanted to stay at the Church albergue in Granon that day and knew there were limited places. This was a "donativo" hostel where, rather than the hostpitalero charging the usual 10 euros, pilgrims donated what they could or wanted to. We walked fast all morning, barely stopping for breaks. We had had coffee and croissant in the bar at Azofra before leaving and this sustained us. We were so determined to make good progress that we did not even stop when we got to Santo Domingo de Calzada, completely forgetting that this was the place with the cathedral where a live cockerel was kept in the nave as a reminder of an old story concerning dishonesty and disbelief. We regretted our omission later, but at the time we were on a walking roll. We met a pilgrim of a similar age to us and walked with her for a while. Francoise was from France and was walking as far as Leon on this occasion but hoping to return in the autumn to complete the pilgrimage. Francoise' English was very good, so all three of us could freely converse. We saw our first storks as we walked beyond Santo Domingo de Calzada. They were building nests on tall industrial chimneys. We were delighted to see them as we had never seen storks in the wild before.

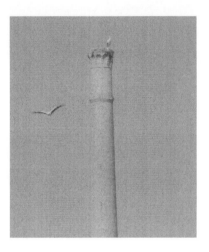

We were amongst the first to arrive in Granon, the Canadians Susie and Cecelia beating us in. This hostel was one of the quirkiest we stayed at on our pilgrimage. The hostel was behind and above the church. Pilgrims all slept together on mats on the attic floor and ate together in the room below. As we had got in early we were able to access the one shower easily – the queue became bigger later. We went to a bar in the village, found a shop for a few provisions, sat in the sun, chatted to other pilgrims – it was lovely. We knew we could not manage the type of racing-walking we had done that day all that often so Jane decided to try and phone a private hostel in Villambistia to secure the following night's accommodation. This involved getting all the necessary phrases written out beforehand in Spanish (I am an English Pilgrim. I do not have much Spanish. Can you speak English? May I have two beds for tomorrow night? My name is …).

And it worked. Jane was reassured when the man at the other end very clearly repeated "Si, dos camas para manana". Job done; there would now be no worries about tomorrow's accommodation.

Enjoying the sun before mass and communal meal

As this was a church albergue, the evening meal would be served after evening mass. We decided to attend mass, along with the majority of the other pilgrims in the hostel and many of the local villagers. This was a Tuesday and if it was a particular feast day, it was not clear; none-the-less the church was quite full – perhaps the villagers are always very devout. The mass, of course, was in Spanish, but we found little resonance with our own memories of attending mass and instead spent the time admiring the grandiose altar piece rising above and behind the altar, very similar to the glittering golden one in Navarette. After the mass the priest asked all pilgrims to step to the front for a pilgrim blessing, which was a rather nice touch. We were now cold and very hungry. Everyone pitched in to set the refectory style tables back in the hostel and the two volunteer hospitaleros proceeded to serve a tasty potato-based sausage stew and salad. We sat with Francoise and Bethany who had both arrived after us. All the young Germans were there as well – none of them gave us odd looks so we guessed they had not worked out that we were the groping grannies. The room was full of chatter in several languages and the jolly volunteers established an upbeat atmosphere.

At the end of the meal but before the communal clear up, washing and drying of dishes, the two volunteers sprung a surprise on us all. They read out from the signing-in book, where we had been asked to give name and nationality, and asked each nationality to stand and sing a song from their country. The Germans were asked to start as they were the largest group and could get confidence in their numbers. As the singing moved from one nationality to another some singers were confidant and very good, others were shy and some were clearly not singers. A young Brazilian man stood in the centre of the room and regaled us with a long melodious and operatic rendition. A young Korean woman gamely sang in her own language. Only an Indian lady declined to sing. Francoise, sitting next to Jane, and the only French person there, could not think what to sing, the Dutch having already sung Frere Jacques in their own language. Jane suggested "Alouette, gentille alouette" which was a good choice as the Canadians all joined in, making it easier for Francoise. Bethany sang the song all American children sang at the beginning of their school day – an oath of allegiance to their flag. As for the two English women – well, our minds went completely blank until Charlotte thought of something we at least both knew the chorus of. Now, Charlotte is a member of a choir in Sheffield and does performances in public, so this communal singing was no problem for her; Jane, by contrast has a voice like a corncrake – so this was a big deal for her. We stood and Charlotte explained we would sing a well-known English folk song in dialect. We launched into Lonny Donegan's "My Old Man's a Dustman" in cockney accents.

We sang the chorus about our "old man" being a dustman and about his wearing a dustman's hat. We sang about his "cor-blimey" trousers and that he lived in a council flat. We explained that he looked like a proper "narner" in his huge boots and that he used the cockney rhyming slang term "daisy roots" to describe them. As one we both realised that we only remembered the chorus so we sang it again. By this time the audience had got the hang of it and were joining in. We improvised a bit, repeated a bit, held onto our imaginary braces and threw in a few "oi s" for good measure and it seemed to go down well, with everyone clapping along with us -- phew! After the grand clear up, we went to bed.

That night at Granon on the thin little mats was the most uncomfortable of the whole pilgrimage. It is probable that few of us slept very well, although some people must have as there was a fair bit of snoring. Whilst it was a relief to get up in the morning, we were both very pleased to have had this unusual experience – but we felt it was the type of experience to keep limited. A simple breakfast of coffee and bread was provided. We gave our donation and set off with full wet weather gear as it was pouring with rain.

Day 14. May 15th Granon – Villafranca Montes de Oca 15.9K then 12K in taxi as booked albergue at Villambistia closed (stayed at albergue attached to Hotel San Anton Abad)

This day was to prove quite a trying day, but we were now becoming better at dealing with the challenges that beset us. We were in our over-trousers and cagoules all day. It was very cold, wet and windy. There was no view. We did pause and risk taking the camera out as we passed from Rioja into the province of Castille y Leon, the largest of the provinces we had to walk through. A huge sign indicating the towns and villages in Castille y Leon ensured we did not miss the moment we stepped from one province to another.

As we walked we became aware that our base layers were getting very wet. We thought at first the rain was blowing in around our hoods and dribbling under our cuffs and up our sleeves. In fact we decided that our incredibly light weight cagoules were not up to the combination of rain, wind and very heavy rucksacks. Pilgrims passed us wearing a variety of rain ponchos, some of which appeared to be doing a decent job. We walked with Francoise for a time and her knee length poncho was keeping her top half very dry. Her legs, socks and boots, however were soaking. We walked a bit with Bethany and Jenny. Jenny's poncho was enormous and covered her well, but Bethany was very cold in a very flimsy poncho with no cagoule under it. We knew we had to warm up so we decided to stop at Belorado, about 10 miles into our day's walk. This was the first place with any café or bar. Jane noticed that there was a Tourist Information Office in the central square so we went to ask if there was a shop in the town selling pilgrims' gear as we hoped to buy a poncho to give us added protection and warmth. The young woman gave us detailed instructions that eventually took us way outside the town to a ladies dress shop that was closed – something obviously got lost in the translation! We plodded back to the square to the café and were delighted to find Francoise there sheltering from the weather. We asked her where she was staying and when she told us she hoped to get in where we had booked, we advised she phone the hostel as it had very few places. It was just as well she did as she was emphatically told that they were closed on a Wednesday. When she explained that her friends were booked in for that day, they said we could not be as they were closed. So much for Jane's forward planning from the day before – clearly, "Si, dos camas para manana" did not mean anything of the sort.

We now all had a problem. We were soaking wet and cold. The rain was turning to sleet and snow. It was nearly five miles to Villambistia where we had discovered we could not stay so we would have to walk further. The village after that had a tiny hostel (we later learnt from Bethany and Jenny that it was empty but incredibly creepy) or we could go a further five kilometres from Villambistia to a village where there were two larger hostels. We decided to do this and because we were so wet we decided to catch a bus for those 10 kilometres. In fact we got a taxi as this was the simpler and cheaper option with three of us sharing. The taxi driver told us that the weather that spring in Spain was exceptionally cold and wet and that there could be more snow ahead. We felt that we had made the right decision. We phoned ahead to the hostel, San Anton Abad at Villafranca Montes de Oca to book three beds, crossing our fingers that this time the booking would work. It did. Behind the hotel of the same name was the hostel, set up by the hotel proprietor after he returned from his own pilgrimage. The rain stopped briefly and we were able to drape our clothes around to begin to get them dry. There were around 18 people in our dormitory and there were two dormitories in the hostel.

We went over to the hotel to book a pilgrims menu meal for the evening and to use the pay-computer. Here we bumped into Claude, the French lady we had met at Torres del Rio. We introduced her to Francoise and we all agreed to meet for our evening meal. The two of us then spent a happy period updating our blog.

Hostel at San Anton Abad

Blog (Jane) Wednesday, 15 May 2013 In Sun and In Rain

Yesterday we walked all day in beautiful sunshine and after several hours it even became warm! (yes, I know we are in Spain, but it is flippin´ freezing here!)

Today we walked all day in the rain and got fairly soaked. Up to now we have, as true Lake District walkers, been very dismissive of all the pilgrims with their big rain ponchos that cover both them and their backpacks. Today we were just plain envious. The poncho stops the rain getting onto your pack straps and seeping in through the waterproof. We shall now eat some humble pie (a little bit like tortilla) and buy a poncho each when we can - big problem there as Spain only has vegetable shops and pharmacies and they are always shut!)

News to-date: Night-before-last we stayed at the municipal albergue in Azofra in little two-person cubicles with saloon-type door -- great, but..... When I was returning from the loos in middle of the night after tippy-toeing there (do not know why I crept, the flush was like Niagara Falls! -- I crept back into my room and felt my way to my sleeping bag and, horrors, there was someone in my bed!!!! I do not know who was more surprised, the young German man or me! Quickly beat a retreat to number 7 (I had gone to number 6 in the dark).

Next day (yesterday) we stayed in the Church albergue on mats in a loft along with 20 others in rows on the floor -- what an experience - shades of the Girl Guides, but with more snoring. And that is not all. After mass (!) we all ate a lovely, simple meal together then every nation present was asked to sing a song from their country. Charlotte and I could only come up with the very traditional folksong, sung in dialect "My Old Man's a Dustman"; it went down well. BUT we need your help. If this singing malarkey crops up again, we need some suggestions for short, melodic English songs -- all clean please.

Blog (Charlotte): Jane claims to have made a mistake in the night but I also managed to burst into a shower to find a naked man, oops! This communal living takes some getting used to. We are now at Villa Franca in a very nice albergue run by a man who himself has walked the Camino. He also owns the hotel next door where we shall eat our pilgrim meal this evening. We both got cold today but the sun is now shining so we are hoping tomorrow, which is up and down through beautiful woodland, will be drier than today.

We have seen storks, two nests on two tall chimneys, amazing. Jane took some pics which we will put on the blog with our other flora and fauna pics soon.

The meal that evening with Francoise and Claude was very pleasant. Earlier we had noticed a young woman with an English accent in the hotel lobby very engaged in conversation with a piratical looking French man – much older than her, with a jaunty scarf tied round his head. We assumed they were a couple, but in fact he was in our dormitory and she was elsewhere. Francoise was a little wary of him; she did not say why, just that he came from Marseilles, but perhaps she had overheard something. That evening, whenever he got out of his bunk he would throw a towel over his head – strange. The following morning he did the same towel-on-head routine, but it slipped. The reason for the jaunty, piratical head-scarf and the towel became apparent – male pattern baldness. From worrying that he might be taking advantage of a young English girl, we became a little sympathetic – it can be as difficult for a man as for a woman to accept the ravages of time. Later we would see them walking together but he had an ancient bike and was wearing a very old motor bike helmet so we guessed they would be parting company at some point.

We did feel a little protective towards the young women walking on their own. We finally saw this particular young woman towards the end of the pilgrimage tucking into a cooked breakfast and on her own; clearly she had managed.

Before going to supper we had walked down to the only obvious shop for a few provisions and found two very cheap and cheerful plastic ponchos. Well, we thought we had won the lottery! Sorted!

Day 15. May 16th Villafranca Montes de Oca – Ages   16K/10M (stayed at El Pajar de Ages)

The day started at 06.00 as walkers started getting up and out. This was the day we first met the mud. We were out by 07.35 having eaten a banana and drunk some water. We had three hills to climb that day, so, although the total planned distance was short, we knew we would have to dig into our stamina reserves. Henry texted us clearly worried about the three climbs we had to do and probably imagining some of the steep narrow paths one gets in the Lake District. He knew that both of us suffered from vertigo on precipitous inclines. The previous day we too had been worried, especially as we thought that the weather might get even colder as we got higher. The reality of our three climbs was very different. Much of the path we climbed up was broad enough for two cars to comfortably pass each other; clearly the forestry vehicles used the paths as the many ruts testified. Whilst the first climb was steep, it was technically just a plod only made a little more difficult as we had to wend our way around the huge puddles and muddy areas left from the previous day's bad weather. We were glad to get to the top of the first ascent where there was a large war memorial dedicated to the fallen of the Spanish civil war. We ate a couple of biscuits and took off again. The day was very cold but the rain and sleet held off despite the threateningly cloudy sky. We even had the very occasional sunny spell. The scenery that day was different as we were mostly walking through forestry woodland so we did not have the big distant vistas we had become accustomed to. As with many climbs one has to go down before having to climb up again, which is exactly what we did for the second of the day's climbs. This was less arduous than the first, but Charlotte had now got Jane's cold so we had to stop many times to catch breath, blow noses or wait for each other.

There were quite a few pilgrims on the route today, including the tiny Indian woman who had not wanted to sing at Granon. She was walking on her own and at one point was merrily marching in the wrong direction. It took quite a few of us all bellowing at her to get her to turn round and realise her error. It was just as well it was not one of the days when there was no one else around as in this forest the paths all looked pretty much the same and she might have been walking for a long time before realising her error.

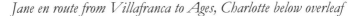

Jane en route from Villafranca to Ages, Charlotte below overleaf

We girded our loins for the final ascent, but having done the pre-requisite descent to a tiny river, the ascent was then barely deserving of that title. All of a sudden we found we must have done the climb without realising because we found that we were descending into the hamlet of St Juan de Ortega. We had managed our three ascents and it had not been too bad. Now it was "downhill all the way" to the village of Ages, where we would try our luck for a bed.

We tried the first place we came to, but the proprietor told us he was closed. We tried a place a little further into the village and were asked if we had booked. Jane made a mental note that she had to crack this booking business. On hearing we had not booked the receptionist asked us to wait. He disappeared for some time, but eventually returned to say yes, we could have two beds. He gave us paper sheets to put over the mattress and showed us to an empty room. We each took a bottom bunk and stowed our stuff in lockers provided. Very rapidly the room filled up entirely with a group of French people and Francoise. The large group had only just started walking and were only doing a few days before returning home. We found them a little strange as the women had rather ostentatious massages given by one of the men, whilst only in their knickers – we felt a little like using the youth expression "get a room".

It was bitterly cold and also windy so we went to sit in a local bar, have a coffee and an orange juice and planned the themes we would write our blogs around. The barman, on passing us on one occasion as we nursed our one drink and availed ourselves of the warmth in his bar, suddenly gave us two little cakes from his bar and tapped his nose. What a nice man! On returning to the albergue to use the pay computer in the narrow little hallway, we found Bethany and Jenny had arrived. They were getting permission to use the albergue's washing machine to wash almost all their gear as over the past two days they had got much of their stuff wet and muddy. It was lovely to see them but we were concerned to hear that after we had parted on the wet and snowy day, they had not stopped at Belorado as we had, but had carried on to the village beyond Villambistia. Bethany had got so wet and cold she was fearful she could not continue. They had found an albergue that appeared not to be open, but a very creepy man had let them stay. They had both been very worried and were glad not to be on their own in that place, but had each other for company. We had booked both supper and breakfast at the hostel and we all ate a not especially nice paella together that evening.

Blog (Jane) Thursday, 16 May 2013 The Pilgrim Menu

Hi Everyone! I know we said we'd write about flora and fauna, but we've had a special request from Maria to write about Spanish food (I think Maria may believe it is not as good as Italian; she may be correct!)

Anyway, we are actually eating very well. Usually we have to be a bit independent in the mornings as bars are not always open and most hostels don't provide breakfast. A banana, bread and water is the normal start then we stop for coffee as soon as we find a bar -- maybe not for many miles. Lunch is a cheese and tomato sandwich prepared the day before. Yesterday when we were frozen and wet and discovered the hostel we'd booked in at was in fact closed, we had tortilla-- delicious! It gave us the energy and courage we needed to sort our problem out. We ended up in a lovely hostel, behind a 3 star hotel and run by the man who owned the hotel who wanted to give something back to pilgrims having done The Way himself when younger.

In the evenings we tend to eat The Pilgrim Menu, which is offered by many bars and restaurants in the towns and villages (not the cities, I think). It ranges from 9 to 12 euros. Sometimes you get a choice of dishes for the three courses, sometimes you get what you're given. So it is vegetable soup, or mixed salad, or pasta of some sort. This is followed by fish, pork, chicken, meatballs -- always with chips. This is followed by yoghurt, ice cream, rice pudding, the ubiquitous Spanish flan (crème caramel), etc. Bread, red wine and water are all included (never white wine -- shame!) Portions can be huge, so unlikely to be losing weight!

We haven't yet experienced tapas or any other traditional foods; perhaps we will when we have our rest day at Burgos on Saturday. Oops, I forgot! Charlotte had a fish soup in Logroño - full of many sea creatures. She said it was delicious - I just had to believe her.

These were enormous bags of live snails being sold in a greengrocer shop. So, if we get desperate, we can always scrounge along the hedgerows! Anyway, I think we can safely say that Maria's reputation as la bellissima cuoca is quite safe.

PS I nearly forgot! We have been walking now for over two weeks and have done over 160 miles! (H. will probably correct me on my additions!) Only one sore toe between us -- Charlotte's, and that is only a little one.

We had been very complacent about our absence of serious injury, congratulating each other on how the "slow and steady" approach was working. We had been pleased with how our daily regimen of unctions and lotions was working to keep us going. Well, as the proverb says: "pride comes before the fall. This is exactly what was going to happen to us in the weeks ahead.

CHAPTER SEVEN   THE ROUGH WITH THE SMOOTH

Day 16. May 17th Ages – Burgos 22K/14M (Stayed at Meson del Cid)

The following thirteen days of our pilgrimage were to confront us with a mixture of emotions and challenges. We thought we were really getting on top of being pilgrims; becoming stronger and more accepting of the various people and places we met. We felt we were dealing well with the changing circumstances and whilst remaining home-sick at times, we were absolutely sure we would complete the pilgrimage. We had no blisters. The aches and pains we felt each day seemed to be responding to our daily treatment of arnica cream and anti-inflammatory gel so that each day we were ready to walk again. We had seen many people limping from blisters or torn muscles, but our slow and steady approach seemed to be doing the trick. However, we needed to be more heedful that life could spring surprises and force compromises. The old adage about taking every day as it came was to become quite pertinent.

That morning's walk from Ages was to throw a different type of challenge at us. We thought we had met mud the previous day, but it was nothing to what we had to squelch through on this day. That morning we made a slow start as we were not in a hurry; Henry had booked us a hotel for two nights in Burgos. The two of us together with Francoise were the last down to breakfast. The hostpitalero had left bread and jam, fruit juice and coffee in flasks out the night before. We were disappointed to find the French blokes from our room filling up their flasks with the coffee that was supposed to be available for everyone. (Clearly after all that massaging, they needed more than their fair share of fortification!) The three of us only just managed to scrape a small cup each. It was pouring with rain outside so we donned full wet-weather gear including the new plastic ponchos. We discovered they were cheap for a very good reason. Charlotte's ripped immediately and it was obvious they were not going to keep us warm. We did have great fun taking photos of each other however, and felt there was a possible theme for a blog on Camino fashion.

This is Charlotte, looking like Bin-bag Bertha.

Jane -- "The bells! The bells! Must see the Osteopath when I get back.

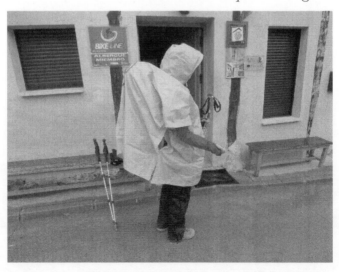

We had a long slog up a hill on the Sierra Atapuerca before descending on a long mud slip of a path. Thank goodness for the walking poles! As we have said before, downhills create their own challenges, but when one has to slurp one's foot out of the clinging mud at each step, zigzag all over the path looking for a slightly less bad route through, pry the weight of mud off one's boots periodically when walking became impossible, endlessly twist and wobble to prevent falling into the mud – the walking poles were an essential. It was very slow and tiring walking. We came to a small village after the descent where we cleaned our boots at a fountain before going to a bar for coffee and tortilla – our new favourite pick-you-up.

We had read in our guide book that the approach to Burgos was four miles of dreary suburb and the advice was to consider taking a bus from Castanares. A slightly more direct route would take us along the edge of the major trunk road into Burgos. We decided to take the path to Castanares. This required walking along dirt paths next to fields with crops in and around the perimeter of the airfield. Dirt paths are fine normally, but after the recent rain they were a complete quagmire. Once more we squelched and slipped our way along, periodically resorting, for a little respite, to walking on the edges of the fields. We still feel guilty for walking in the fields as we are believers in the country code and sympathetic to the hard work of those people who have to prise their livelihood from the land, but mud walking is so utterly exhausting.

After ten kilometres of this wearisome mud walking we arrived at Castanares, part of the extensive Burgos suburbs. As we looked a filthy sight we stripped off all our wet weather gear that was by now plastered with mud and we spent some time locating the correct bus stop. Whilst standing at the bus stop a man and woman approached us and asked whether we were going to Burgos and that if we were, we could have a lift in their car. As if she had not spent two weeks on a pilgrimage Jane's mind immediately sprung into its usual anxiety mode: were these people white slavers (as if two women of a certain age would be anybody's obvious first choice to abduct), were they muggers (what would a pilgrim be carrying apart from a little cash and dirty spare socks), did they have some other dastardly motive behind their offer? In the meantime, Charlotte had said "yes please" and jumped into the car! These two kind people then proceeded to drive us the four miles into the centre of the city, winding their way through the one-way system to drop us off behind the cathedral. The man had once been a pilgrim and asked us to say a prayer for him in Santiago. As a result of this kindness, we arrived in Burgos early with an afternoon to do laundry, explore and find a shop that sold proper ponchos.

The glorious view of the cathedral from our hotel window

We had been given instructions and a map by the hotel receptionist showing us how to find a sports equipment shop. We walked a long way and had just decided we would walk only one more block before turning round, when, just as the receptionist had indicated, we found the shop in a not particularly upmarket part of the sprawling town. At first sight it did not look promising - lots of T-shirts and trainers. However, on a little balcony above the main shop was a rack of ponchos. Now people wearing ponchos do tend to look a little odd, particularly with a large backpack under the poncho. Clearly the manufacturers of the ponchos we bought felt that the discrete colours of florescent orange and lime green would help the wearers blend into their surroundings. You can judge for yourselves when you see the photos. Notwithstanding the interesting colours, these ponchos were to prove very useful in the days ahead. They did keep the weather out and we could unzip them down the front and wear them as fashion statement cloaks draped over our packs when the weather was changeable.

Very relieved to have solved the problem of how to keep dry and warm we returned to the centre to have a coffee, buy some postcards for the grandchildren and visit the famous cathedral.

Day 17. May 18th Rest day in Burgos

Blog (Jane): Burgos is a lovely city and as Henry had found an ideal location for us we were able to watch from the window traditional Spanish wedding dancing and brides galore having photos taken with the cathedral as their backdrop. The dancing and singing was brilliant (short video for you lucky people who will be invited to our Camino Way meal and slide show!). The dancing was extremely characterful. All the musicians and dancers were in traditional dress. The dancers held and played castanets and danced around the bride and groom who stood (shivering) in the centre of the circle. All the guests and passers-by stood and clapped or skipped in time to the music. It all felt and looked very Spanish.

All around the city are statues - old people sitting on benches, a policeman directing traffic, a pilgrim nursing sore feet and so on.

This was a bit of a busman's holiday for Charlotte (formerly working with people with dementia) and I had to tear her away eventually when the two old dears refused to remember the words " apple, table, penny".

You can see the pilgrim's backpack with cockle shell (we all have cockle shells dangling off our packs to show we are pilgrims).

We had been a little nervous about how we would feel in Burgos after the less than happy experiences in Logroño, but we loved Burgos. The centre was clean, interesting and picturesque. We saw many familiar faces as we wandered around. It was usually easy to spot an "off duty" pilgrim as, if they were not wearing their boots they would often be wearing Crocs – a very light weight "about town" shoe. We met Susie and Cecelia in the cathedral admiring the myriad artistic marvels. One's eye was very much drawn to heaven in the cathedral and the best way, if one wanted to avoid a terrible crick in the neck was to lie on a pew and gawp at the wonders. Charlotte did not do that and suffered the consequences that evening; having trapped a nerve she got bouts of giddiness – thank goodness for our anti-inflammatory gel!

Blog (Jane) Saturday, 18 May 2013 (rest day) Where we rest our weary heads We thought you might like to learn a little about where we have been staying and the life in pilgrim hostels. Actually, as pampered pilgrims we have now interspersed our albergue stays with three hotels (four if you count where we flew into). It took us some time to get into hostel rituals and routines but we have pretty much got it sussed now. We can pack our rucksacks in the dark, which it often is at 06.00. It takes a brave soul to turn the light on even when it is obvious there is only one lazy so-and-so still in bed. Then the stampede for the bathroom facilities begins - these facilities can be minimal. This whole routine can start even earlier as there are groups of very early risers (are they walking 40 K or are they determined to get the two sheets of toilet paper that are left in the one toilet?) You lie in bed, watching the torch-light show and listening to the dry sacks rustling as people try to creep out and in fact everybody is just being woken up!

We often stay in large mixed dormitories and the snoring can fairly rattle the Windows. Earplugs are an essential Camino Way accessory. One of the lovely things about this communal living is the camaraderie that can develop and it is great when later you bump into those familiar faces. Here are a few pics of places we have stayed. (See next page)

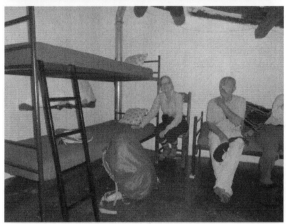

Hostels at: Uterga, Lorca and Granon

During our stay in Burgos, we completed all our small commissions: bought the ponchos, donated the plastic yellow ones to the municipal albergue, bought a few provisions and postcards, wrote up the blog, caught up on the Spanish weather forecast on the TV – it did not look brilliant - washed absolutely everything with the exception of fleeces and cagoules, found a lovely coffee and cake shop, bumped into Bethany and Jenny and really enjoyed our rest period. The hotel itself was in need of an uplift, but we were becoming more blasé about grubby porcelain. The breakfast choice was amazing and the food delicious – we felt very spoilt. The weather was threatening and often rainy. We watched a spectacular thunder and lightning storm from the hotel window and felt sorry for all the brides in the freezing weather. (We had a bird's eye view of many wedding photo shoots – clearly the cathedral is a popular backdrop for wedding party photos.)

We met a delightful couple, Terrence and Kate, at the hotel and had dinner with them. Kate had already done the Camino Way and was back doing research for the university she worked at in Australia. She told us that they had re-visited a spot where, when she had been doing the walk on her own three years earlier, she had climbed high above a gulf where there was a spectacular view. She had taken her sleeping bag out of her pack to get her camera and was juggling the camera and sleeping bag on the precipitous edge when she dropped the sleeping bag. Now, a sleeping bag becomes a very precious item on a pilgrimage like this, but Kate had had this particular bag for very many years since her youth and had shared many exciting journeys with it. She was distraught. There was no way she could retrieve it from the chasm below, so she stood and wept as if she had lost a loved one. Clearly she was still grieving for her bag. They did not find it when they re-visited the spot. We were sad to say goodbye to them both the following morning, but we were all geared up for the next phase of our walk as we would soon be walking across the Meseta.

Day 18. May 19th Burgos to Hornillos del Camino 21K/13.1M (stayed at municipal albergue)

Because we had breakfast at the hotel in Burgos, we did not leave very early. We had seen from our hotel window many pilgrims walking past the hotel much earlier than us. Jane was anxious about getting a bed that night as the tiny village of Hornillos del Camino was the obvious stopping point for many pilgrims walking out of Burgos; with only one hostel, there would be competition to get a bed. There was one village before that, but it was only 13.3 kilometres from Burgos (about 8 miles). Susie and Cecelia were stopping there as they did not want the uncertainty of getting in at Hornillos. We met up with them in a bar en route where they shared their cake with us. This would be the last time we saw them, although we did not know it at the time. Unless we knew for sure we would not see someone again, we did not say any final goodbyes. There was always an assumption that we would meet again further along the Way. Because we kept meeting many of the same people, in the same hostels or in bars, we came to assume that we would continue to do that. It was only after days or weeks of not meeting up with someone that we realised we would probably never see them again. As we were not Facebook or Twitter people, we did not automatically exchange any contact details, so people came into our lives and then left them. We did not say farewell to Susie or Cecelia that day. We do so hope those intrepid ladies made it to Santiago and on to Finisterre before their visas expired.

For the two of us it would have been a pleasant walk that day but for the continuous rain and Jane's anxiety over the night's lodgings, and Charlotte's continuing dizziness. We usually walked at pretty much the same pace until towards the end of each day when Jane would pick up the pace for a final dash to the hostel. We got pretty much the same enjoyment from the natural delights around us. We found the same people interesting, amusing or irksome. Yes, we could get "scratchy" with each other occasionally, but in a way because we were sisters we could get away with that; we had such a shared history of managing through difficult times that a little bit of annoyance caused by too much proximity was not going to create any irreparable damage. We were discovering that if we did not see eye-to-eye over something, if we just walked quietly the annoyances largely resolved themselves. It is one of the joys of walking, that it creates a natural space for intimacy or distance, depending on one's mood. It is so much easier to talk about a difficult or personal topic as one is walking across a fell or through the countryside as one's walking companion can stop for a breather, point out some bit of scenic beauty, change the subject, respond or not – all in a more natural way than if one is sitting face-to-face in a bar or sitting room. Having said that, for most of our walking on the Camino Way we were talking about the practical logistics of the journey, or commenting on the immediacy of our surroundings. We had not talked about what to do with a life of retirement or how to build and maintain feelings of independent self-worth. We were neither of us having any "road to Damascus" insights. We had done a bit of singing, which had been something Charlotte was hoping to teach Jane, but usually there were too many people around to practice much of that – a bonus for the birds and beasts of the Spanish fields.

Blog (Jane): Back on The Way- guess what-- in the rain. Cue fashion shoot!

This is us in our new ponchos (thank you Burgos). We look quite normal from the front, but check out the side view! Honey Monster eat your heart out! (We donated the other, plastic ones to an Albergue. Not sure we were doing anyone any favours!)

Anyway, they worked. Although you do tend to develop your own micro-climate in there. Despite the fairly poor weather, it was a good day's walking in fresh air and the rain let up periodically.

The rain receded as we approached Hornillos, a tiny, one street village with one small shop, a bar, the municipal albergue and a sports hall. Hornillos was not our favourite place. We were grateful that we found a bed for the night as the weather was very threatening and it was cold; we did not want to walk another six kilometres to the next village. However, given the numbers of pilgrims that pour into the village one would think that both the hostel and the bar would have streamlined their services a little. The reception to the hostel was two flights of stairs down. We all queued with packs on backs and slowly stepped down, one step at a time over a period of an hour. When we eventually got to the receptionist she slowly recorded the full details from our passports and told us to wait outside as there was no space in this hostel. By the time the hospitalero had finished with the pilgrims, a large number of us were congregated on the steps outside. She took us to a building up the street. This was the overflow hostel where one toilet, shower and basin (no lock on the door) served twenty of us. It all needed a thorough clean. The bunk beds were the dirtiest we had experienced so far. We were hugely glad we had our pillow cases so our faces did not have to touch any part of the dirty mattress. Pilgrims who arrived later were shown to the old gym hall. We met a couple in the bar who said it was absolutely freezing there so we took them back to our room and gave them the blanket off the end of our bunks – there was no way we were going to use these dirty-looking blankets ourselves. We asked the girls to return them in the morning. We had a sense at this stage that the month of May on the Camino Way was not the quiet month we had understood it would be from our earlier research, but in fact was very popular. Jane decided to try booking ahead so we would not have to spend the whole of each day's walk in a state of anxiety. For some pilgrims the open-endedness of each day is part of the delight of the walk. For us we realised that we had not built up the additional stamina to cope with days too much longer than 20 – 22 kilometres.

Day 19. May 20th   Hornillos del Camino – Castrojeriz 20.2K/12.6M (stayed at El Camping)

We had not slept well at Hornillos, partly because we kept imagining creepy crawlies climbing on us from the dirty surroundings, partly because Charlotte kept getting prodded by the woman opposite her to stop her snoring (although the Japanese man above was making at least as much noise) and partly because Jane needed to get up three times that night and with no ladder that was a tricky expedition each time. We became part of the "rustle-and-dash" brigade as we got up at 05.30. We gathered together all our stuff in the dark and carried it outside where we packed and put on our boots in a little side room. We were so happy to be out in the cold fresh air and to watch the beautiful sunrise; we were walking on the Meseta by 06.20.

We had read about the Meseta before embarking on the pilgrimage. The guide book described it as "sublime" and we came to agree with that. Others found the Meseta flat and wearisome and we had read of pilgrims simply taking the train or bus from Burgos to Leon in order to miss out the Meseta altogether. Whilst it was to prove a challenge to us, we are glad we did not think of skipping it. The Meseta is a high plateau in central Spain and we would be walking across the higher northern part of it – around 900 metres high (or approximately 3000 feet) – a similar altitude to the highest English mountains. It is described as largely treeless and windblown, blisteringly hot in summer and freezing in winter and is sparsely populated. As we left Burgos we had at first found the terrain rolling and interesting. This continued on the second day of walking across this high plateau as we walked down to Hontanas and up to Castrojeriz. We continued to see vibrant and diverse wild flowers on the field verges, including huge clumps of wild rocket with their little white and brown flowers – deliciously sharp to nibble on. The rain held off but we wore our cagoules for warmth.

Because we had started walking that morning at 06.20, we arrived at El Camping before 12.00 and found our booking ahead had worked – well it worked in part. We got a room but then had to give it up and take a smaller one when another party arrived who had a prior claim. The room we had booked was part of a camping complex on the edge of the village of Castrojeriz and was run by an extremely lovely Spanish chap and his son. Despite it being very cold, the sun had come out so we did washing and strung it out on a clothes line outdoors to dry whilst we went to explore. From the village we could see the hill we would have to climb the following day before moving into the flat Meseta proper. There were several hostels in the village so it is probable that we would have found a bed without having to book ahead. We were both very tired following the night at Hornillos so whilst Charlotte had a nap, Jane updated the blog on the pay computer at El Camping.

That evening we had a delicious meal at the campsite along with a few other people who were camping there. Charlotte did some needlework improvements to her walking trousers so that she could roll up the legs and keep them fixed up with a button to avoid the worst of the mud. (Jane had zipped off the bottom of her trousers as it was better to have cold legs rather than getting the bottoms filthy each day – we only washed the walking trousers very periodically.) We had taken one of those little hotel courtesy needlework packs with us and it had proved very useful. Jane had taken in the waist of both her pairs of trousers (they were too big to start with) and Charlotte used the two little buttons in the kit to customise her trousers. Another useful little thing we had brought with us was some duct tape that we had wound round the tops of our walking poles. This acted as an identifier for the poles but we had also used it to repair the plastic ponchos before donating them in Burgos and to mend the anti-inflammatory gel tube that had become punctured somehow.

Blog (Jane) Monday, 20 May 2013

Today was a lovely walk and we even had some sunshine towards the end of the walk. We booked ahead and got a room with shared access to a proper bathroom (all part of a campsite complex) and with very kindly helpful Spanish people.

(More on that in a later blog, but we are finding some of the Spanish to be a little like Europe's Yorkshire folk – a bit brusque.)

In contrast to the lovely statues in Burgos, the rural ones are a little more primitive!

Town and Country Mice - Charlotte is having a snooze in our room at El Camping so I am whiling away some time blogging. Friday afternoon and Saturday we stayed in the beautiful city of Burgos. Sunday and today, Monday we have begun walking on the Spanish Meseta, a very high plateau that one reads much about. In summer it can be very hot with little shade; in autumn it can be uniformly brown. However, in spring it is verdant green with many hedgerow flowers and, at this early stage of our long walk across it, it is varied and undulating. Oops, I forgot to mention -- it can be muddy - an abiding motif at the moment.

Blog (Charlotte) Monday, 20 May 2013 None So Queer As Folk

Charlotte. I am now awake having had a snooze, I was going cross eyed due to lack of sleep. We thought we would tell you about some of the people we have encountered along the Way. We have said before that one of the extraordinary aspects of this journey is the brief friendships that are formed each day, some last a few days as our paths criss-cross. We have some pictures of the most memorable and lovely pilgrims we have spent time with but some we did not get pictures of, for instance two lovely Canadian men, Leo and Bill whom we met in Orrison and also Cecelia and Susie two seventy year olds who are walking from Le Puy in France. We are still crossing paths with them.

(In the blog we wrote on that day we included the photos of a number of our transient Camino friends, but as we did not ask their permission at the time to publish their photos we have now removed them for the purposes of this book.)

An early friend was Ingo who was from Germany and whom we met at Biarritz and who we shared a taxi with into Bayonne and whom we met again in Orrison. He was very friendly, travelling on his own and made us feel confident in making friends along the Way. We assume he is streaks ahead of us now.

Another friend was Darren from South Africa, our lovely companion whom we crossed the Pyrenees with. He was worried about doing this bit on his own and called us the "English Ladies". We are still following him on his blog when we can, however he is definitely following us geographically!

We first met Ayn and Michael from the USA in our posh hotel in Pamplona and our journey forward coincided with them for some days; they were very funny, friendly people and it was always a pleasure to meet up with them. They had sent all their cold weather clothing back home and were regretting their decision as the weather was so much colder than they had anticipated. We assume they are ahead of us as we have not bumped into them again.

Francoise and Claude were both French women travelling on their own and we met up with them individually and then we all met up at a lovely Albergue at Villafranca; Jane had great opportunity to speak French. Francoise had very good English but Claude had none. They are both ahead of us as Francoise was speeding towards Leon and Claude took a train to Sarria. Though a transient meeting we really connected with Francoise in particular and it was sad to say goodbye.

We met up with Bethany and Jenny several times. Bethany from Hawaii was travelling on her own and we first encountered her walking out from Roncesvalles. Her pack had been so heavy that the Pilgrim's Office in St. Jean advised her not to attempt to carry it. She was having it portered till she could post a huge parcel back home. Bethany was a vivacious, funny, charming person who made friends easily and called us "The British Ladies". We bumped into her many times along our way. She met up and travelled with Jenny from Germany, a kindred spirit. But both are now walking separately due to their own personal timetables. We have had many a laugh with these two and we are still seeing Jenny now and again.

Our latest encounter was in Burgos at the hotel. Terrance and his wife Kate from Australia were at breakfast and we thought they were British until Jane spoke to Terrance. They were both academics researching cultural aspects of the Camino Way for their Universities. Kate had travelled the CW herself in 2010. They were tremendous fun; we had our last evening meal with them and it was, we all agreed, delightful. Two incredibly interesting folk it was hard to say goodbye to and in other circumstances we could imagine long-term friendship would/could form.

These are some of the more significant encounters. We also have fleeting conversations, e.g. a lad, Lee, from Telford today, who packed his job in and is walking the CW and then continuing to Lisbon. His journey was inspired by "The Way", Martin Sheen's film. In contrast there have been a few po-faced unfriendly people; we cannot help but wonder why they are on the CW!

Relaxing in Castrojeriz

Day 20. May 21ˢᵗ Castrojeriz –Boadillo del Camino 19.2K/12M (stayed at En El Camino albergue)

We started rather slowly that day as we had a breakfast of coffee and toast at the campsite, but we were reasonably confident we would find a bed at Boadillo del Camino as Jane had booked ahead. (It was always a gamble as to whether or not she had been understood on the phone.) We were pleasantly surprised at how quickly the claggy mud dried out despite the temperature remaining very cold. Charlotte tore herself away from the numerous blue-eyed cats that lived around the campsite and we set off to walk through the village and climb the Alto Mostelares – a short, sharp ascent.

It was bitterly cold at the top so we did not hang about. We had a splendid view of the Meseta rolling out ahead of us. How could anyone say this was not beautiful countryside to walk through? Over the following few days' walking on the Meseta it could become quite daunting at times as destinations were very difficult to gauge. When walking on the flat it was far more difficult to see villages tucked away in little dips or behind clumps of trees. We just had the distant horizon, never seeming to get any closer.

Once we arrived at Boadillo we found the forward booking had indeed worked. It was very much later after our return to England that we read that the hostel we stayed in at Boadillo was one of the much-written-about-and-recommended hostels on the Way. It was lovely: clean, friendly, gloriously bustling and very pilgrim-focused. We talked at breakfast the following morning to an American woman, Raquelle, who had arrived with a fever and she spoke of how caring and solicitous the family who ran the hostel had been. It was an enchanting place. The garden was full of huge pieces of metallic artwork and sculptures. There were benches under a wonderfully perfumed lilac bush. Outside was a tower with three huge stork nests and four storks in residence. In the evening the little square and streets around the hostel were full of swooping, circling swallows and martins. The birds would fly in huge groups and like a local air show, would dive down towards us then suddenly sweep up in unison shooting round the corner of a building to swirl round again. It was a wonder that we did not see little concussed feathery bodies all over the place as they cut their aerobatics very fine. We could feel the air vibrate as the wheeling flocks shot past. We had never seen such displays before.

At dinner that evening we sat opposite Sandra and John, a couple from America. We were always very careful when first talking to people we met in terms of asking about circumstances. Inevitably on a pilgrimage there are people walking who have some sort of sad history of loss or illness. We tended to ask whether people had anyone interested in their pilgrimage progress. If our new companions had family they wanted to talk about, they could tell us if they chose to. When we talked to Sandra and John they told us of the death of their son five years earlier. Sandra told us we were the first people on the pilgrimage that they had freely told this to. She said that if asked how many children she had, she always said two as she could not bear to say only one, but on this occasion she risked revealing their changed circumstances. They had lost their son in an accident when he was a teenager and had not yet come to terms with their loss. They had embarked on the pilgrimage as a way of trying to address their abiding sorrow. They recognised they wanted to move on with life positively as their remaining child, a daughter, had been very close to her brother and was having her own difficulties coping with her loss, leave alone having to help her parents deal with theirs. They were a lovely, seemingly cheerful couple who worked as teachers and touched our hearts deeply. We very much felt after this that we should constantly be counting our blessings.

One of the things Jane did whilst at the Boadillo hostel was to book ahead at the next two planned destinations, so confidence was high and anxiety levels low as we set out the following morning.

Day 21. May 22nd Boadilla del Camino – Villacazar de Sirga 20.9K/13.1M (stayed at Casa Aurea)

It was still bitterly cold and rather overcast, but we started with a pleasant walk beside a wide canal. This was the first day of really flat walking.

We walked along the side of a canal for the six kilometres into Fromista, a small town where we posted cards to the grandchildren and stopped for a coffee. From here we started walking on the infamous "senda", a gravel path created for pilgrims to walk on that runs beside many of the long stretches of wide highway running through Castille y Leon. We had read that the senda is monotonous and that the views are spoilt by the proximity of major roads. However, we found the senda perfectly acceptable; it was just another type of track and at least we did not have to worry about where to walk and we could walk side by side and chat easily. There was relatively little traffic on the roads and we could appreciate the fields stretching out with their undulating crops on all sides. Many fields in fact, were ploughed but not yet growing anything; others had some sort of grain crop already established. What we did not see was any livestock. We occasionally saw huge hangar-type barns in the fields with muck heaps outside and we guessed that these must house cows or pigs. It seemed a shame the beasts had to be kept like that. The only large live creature we saw was a deer that bounded across the road and leapt away across a cereal crop field.

Following the advice in our guide book, we took a diversion from the senda to walk alongside a river for twelve kilometres (7.5 miles). This was a delightful part of the day and we got into a steady and quite fast rhythm. Ever since we had climbed over the Pyrenees three weeks earlier we had heard the distinctive cuckoo call every single day. As we briskly walked beside this river we continuously heard the cuckoo again, but on this occasion it was very close. We stopped and sat for a while on the river bank to rest and look at the bird life around us. To our joy we spotted one of these drab and importunate cuckoos, flying to and fro over what it must have determined was its territory. Unfortunately we were not able to get the camera out in time. We saw storks and feral cats in the fields, presumably all looking for small rodents to eat. We had hoped to stop at the bar at Villovieco indicated in our guide book but when we got there it was clearly closed. We were not really surprised as we appeared to be the only pilgrims that had taken this diversion-from-the-senda route; there really was not the passing custom available to run a business. We stopped for water and a snack and Charlotte used the halt as an opportunity to rub some gel on her shins which were playing up a bit.

The sun did not emerge until long past mid-day but it made us appreciate how important it was to walk early rather than late. We arrived at the delightful village of Villacazar de Sirga in the early afternoon and found our accommodation on the far side of the village. Only one other person was in the room we were allocated so we were able to take the remaining two single beds. We were in a small dormitory behind the bar it belonged to. There was space for only seven people and all beds were taken in due course. There was a small sun-trap garden outside so we did laundry and went to explore. The guide book had said the Knights Templar church of Santa Maria was not to be missed and it gave the two opening times each day. We ended up returning for both these opening times and simply found locked doors all round. Clearly it was not intended that we should visit churches on this pilgrimage.

It was also difficult to buy provisions in Villacazar. There was a tourist type shop open which was fine if you wanted expensive gift wrapped chocolates or glass jars of jam and there was a tiny all-purpose shop that opened very briefly in the evening and only sold its goods in huge packs. We had noticed that many of the little shops on the Way, even in some of the larger towns, sold things individually. Some even sold small travel-sized packs of things like sun cream or shampoo. Clearly the buyers for these shops were attempting to cater for the needs of the pilgrim who only wants to buy small items as everything adds to the weight that has to be carried. In Villacazar it was different; a pack of a dozen eggs and a huge loaf or nothing. We ate that evening in the bar and used the bar computer to write a short blog.

We liked Villacazar. We loved the funny statue of an elderly pilgrim sitting at a table with his tankard of beer. There were many statues of pilgrims along the route, but this was a quaintly comical one. We chatted to John and Peter, two ex-army Brits now living in Spain and walking just part of the Way and a mother and daughter walking the Way while the daughter waited to take up her university place. We met a German chap, Hubert, of a similar age to us. He had very little English but made up for that with his extraordinarily loud snoring at night. We were to meet up a few more times and he always seemed to be delighted to see us. Hubert was having terrible difficulty with blisters. Once again we felt a little smug at our absence of injury – oh the hubris of this smugness!

Blog (Jane) Wednesday, 22 May 2013   Lists and Gracias, Merci, Grazie, Thank You, Thank You!

We both feel really remiss as we have not yet said any thank-yous for all the kind and funny comments you have all been leaving for us. We loved the song suggestions (in fact Charlotte had already been singing the Hippopotamus song as she trudged through the mud), and thank you Eddie and Mark for giving us the full words. We feel very connected with home when reading the comments. We appreciate the efforts you've made to put comments on as we understand it can be a bit complicated. Unfortunately, we cannot always read the comments when you post them; it very much depends on whether the computer system is state-of the art or from-the-ark. However, we catch up when we can.

Top Gear: There are some things we just would not be without on this trip:

Walking poles, obviously as it is not just the two ancient women who have to cover the mileage; it is also those flippin' packs. The poles really do help save the back, legs, hips, sanity. They are so important that after about 100 kilometres we had to purchase specialist attachments. As good pilgrims we had been holding up our poles through all the urban areas and all the villages as they make a terrible click-clack noise on tarmac. This courtesy was doing no end of damage to our backs. We then fell across a little shop (yes, it was open!) and we bought rubber bungs that can be put on and pulled off the end of the poles very easily. We are now the silent pilgrims through all built-up areas.

Pillow cases from home -- lovely for keeping goodness only knows what from ones face, but also they are a bit of home.

Ear plugs and black-out masks -- give some chance of catching a little sleep in the mixed dorms.

Ponchos -- well say no more -- you've seen them!

In fact, everything is important and increasingly dear to us. There are couple of things we have yet to use. Charlotte is still looking for a horse that needs a stone removed from its hoof, and both of us have failed to find the courage to use our she-wees.

Top flora and fauna

At the moment we are blown away by the storks, the size of some of their nests, the bizarre locations of those nests and their clacking courtship rituals. We are accompanied most days by the sound of cuckoos and today actually saw one perched in a tree. The swifts and swallows in the evenings perform aerial acrobatics, sweeping en mass to the ground and around buildings like some sort of Red Arrows team.

The variety of different wildflowers is amazing, but perhaps the best has been the brilliant red, but small poppies and the gorgeous tamarisk trees. We frequently accidently release wild herb scents as we walk as so many herbs, thyme, lavender, rosemary, wild rocket, santolina and others we cannot identify abound on the verges.

We won't mention the Great Peacock moth again, but it is up there at the top of the list.

We have seen relatively few farm animals, but we have a favourite - a Pyrenean Cow, so melancholy and gentle.

Charlotte insists I mention the too-numerous-to-count pretty little, white and ginger feral cats, often with ice blue eyes.

(Posted the following day, 23 May, at Caldadilla): *Photos we forgot*

You have to be very patient and phlegmatic if you are a cow living in the Pyrenees with a huge bell round your neck.

This is a yellow wagtail and boy, was it yellow.

There were three nests on this Church tower in Boadillo and four storks. The male returns to the nest each year and gets it in shape for his mate to arrive. One mate had returned and we watched these enormous and slightly daft birds conduct their courtship dance - which involves much fluffing out of neck ruff feathers and clacking of beaks. You imagine him saying " look at that twig I brought back for the nest. Bet his next door isn´t as big."

Day 22. May 23rd Villacazar de Sirga – Caldadilla de la Cueza 22.7K/14.2M (stayed at Camino Real)

We set off that morning after one of those very rare occurrences – a good night's sleep. This day involved a considerable amount of senda walking. It was extremely cold to start with but we did not stop when we got to the vibrant little town of Carrion de los Condes as we had had breakfast before we left that morning. This day was all about appreciating the views and, for Charlotte, slapping on the anti-inflammatory gel. We saw huge fields sweeping off into the distance. Once we were off the senda and onto a seven mile long gravel track we admired the wild flowers and in the distance caught views of huge mountains. Pilgrims were few and far between. We saw the German boys resting with their hammock strung between two trees, but for the most part we walked alone and quite swiftly. We stopped very infrequently, but did have one rest when we found a picnic table and bench at the side of the track. Charlotte was able to put on more gel. By the time we reached Caldadilla de la Cueza, Charlotte's shins were really beginning to play up and were becoming very painful. We were delighted to discover that the place we had booked from Boadillo had recorded our booking and we were given a lovely room with its own bathroom.

Whilst Jane uploaded some photos onto the blog, Charlotte chatted to Sandra (whom we had met at Boadillo) who advised her on a method of strapping her shins which her own daughter had used when she had got shin-splints (tendonitis) when Scottish dancing. We were just beginning to become a little concerned as we had read extensively about tendonitis before we set out. It could be one of those ailments that scuppered a pilgrim's walk or it could delay progress considerably. We read of some people soldiering on, full to the gunnels with pain-killers, but then taking a very long time to mend once they got home. We hoped that some anti-inflammatory drugs, a good night's rest and suitable strapping would prevent anything too serious from developing.

We sat in the cool sun outside chatting to Jenny and the German boys – Benedict, the big lad, Fabien, the boy with dreadlocks and the hammock and their very shy friend, possibly called Stefan. There were also two much older American men sitting outside – a little like cowboys, regaling everyone on how they had looked after a young woman walking on her own in sandals and who had the worst blisters they had ever seen, all filthy and infected. They seemed like nice guys, but they did like to talk!

Even when walking on the Meseta the hills can be seen in the distance.

Blog (Jane) Thursday, 23 May 2013 The Face of Spain

We have now walked through huge tracts of Spain. We have been through three distinct provinces: Navarre, Rioja and we are now part way through the largest, Castille y Leon. The changes in scenery creep up on one.

This was half way up the Alto del Perdon (The Hill of Forgiveness) on one of our earlier sunny days on 6ᵗʰ May.

On the subject of the face of Spain, we had both embarked on this trip to Spain with a reasonably amount of ignorance about the country, but not a total lack of understanding. Jane had re-read "Homage to Catalonia" by George Orwell and had started on Cervantes' "Don Quixote". Charlotte came from Sheffield, a city from where at least 16 volunteers had gone to take part in the civil war conflict from 1936 – 1939 and was mindful of this connection. In Sheffield Peace Gardens there is a plaque of remembrance for the fallen and for those who fought in Spain, recognising their struggle for democratic principles.

As we walked through Navarre at the beginning of the pilgrimage, we saw on occasion bits of Basque nationalist graffiti, but much of it looked quite old. Later, when we met a Spanish walker, Rafael, he talked to us about the Civil War and its impact on the parts of Spain we were walking through where many of the war dead remained unfound. The Nationalists under Franco and the Republicans had fought bitterly over the key ports and industries in the north and the Basque region. As we all know, the Nationalists eventually gained power in Spain and in many ways this civil war created a European preparedness for the second world war; an aligning of countries - a consolidation of democracies and of fascists. However, as we walked through Spain we had no consciousness of any obvious after effect. We saw only one memorial to the civil war, after Villafranca Montes de Oca. We were mindful that many people who lived in the area will have had family members who had fought on various sides during the civil war; their neighbours may have been on an opposing side. We also knew a little about some of the atrocities that both sides had carried out, with the murder of thousands of prisoners. We appreciated that this could make neighbourly life potentially more difficult – an unquiet past haunting the present.

On an equally sober note, we became very aware of the desertion of rural areas in northern Spain. We walked through some villages that had many empty houses and barns and where the properties had been left to collapse. Occasionally we would see some busy renovation going on of one property amongst a row of dilapidated houses. We were walking along a centuries old route that brought a small amount of prosperity to the places situated along that route, so we wondered what other villages, off the route, must be like in contrast. We had a joke between us that developed after we had seen just one little old lady in an apron cross the road in several seemingly deserted villages. Was she the same old lady or did all little old ladies in aprons look the same? We decided that "Central Casting" must employ her to add authenticity to the Camino villages and they probably drive her around the route to pop up here and there.

There is clearly much unemployment in Spain and Rafael told us that walking the Camino way was a good thing to put on one's curriculum vitae or résumé. However, the towns and cities all appeared to be very vibrant and economically busy with far less of the "empty high street" syndrome that we had in England at that time. In fact, when we stayed in Riego de Ambros on our way down from La Cruz de Ferro, we were told the village was so popular as a summer time retreat for town escapees that the village was virtually a holiday village.

For much of the time the "face of Spain" for us was not especially "Spanish". The trees, the flowers, such animal life that we saw were broadly very familiar. The climate at the time we were walking was also familiar as Spain was having a cold wet spring. Size, however, did make a difference – fields were vast in Castille y Leon, mountains were huge, dogs were big. And, of course meal times were totally un-British!

Day 23. May 24th   Caldadilla de la Cueza – Sahagun 22.7K/14.2M (stayed at Viatoris albergue)

We were out at 07.30 the next day into a bitterly cold morning. Thick frost covered the plants on the verge. Charlotte felt reasonably refreshed so we decided to go on the very slightly longer but more scenic path. No one else appeared to make that decision and once more this was a day when we saw very few pilgrims. It became clear quite quickly that we were going to have to go at a much slower pace as Charlotte's legs were extremely painful. Whilst the going was still very flat, the scenery was far more varied. We saw several little hobbit-type houses built into earth banks – presumably bodegas for storing wine. We saw our first mud and straw building. We heard cacophonous frogs chirping noisily in ditches, we saw beautifully equipped children's play parks – always empty – in the unlikeliest of villages; and, of course, we saw the pastoral vista stretching to the horizon. We raised a cheer when we arrived at Terradillos de Templarios, the half-way point of the pilgrimage. This was an ancient village full of adobe houses and storks. However, our pleasure at reaching this landmark point of our journey was tempered by the increasing pain Charlotte was suffering.

It was obvious to Jane that Charlotte was becoming very distressed both with the pain of the worsening tendonitis, but also at the prospect of what that might mean for the pilgrimage. We stopped for lunch at a bar in a pretty little village where we were joined by one of the American "cowboys" from the previous day. He had a bad knee and had got a lift from a Belgian chap and was now waiting for his friend to arrive. He had been in the transport business back home and spoke knowledgeably about Spanish buses and that there would be no buses on a Sunday and limited transport on a Saturday. We had been hoping to catch a bus in two days' time, on Sunday, from Mansilla de las Mulas into Leon. This was something suggested in the guide book to avoid the long suburb trudge and we thought it would give Charlotte's shins a little recovery time. We now did not know what to do except slowly wend our way to Sahagun, our rest place for that night. However, the "cowboy" had planted a seed in Jane's mind – we had to do whatever it took to keep going – it just was not yet clear what that was.

The germ of an idea was beginning to form in Jane's mind as to how to resolve Charlotte's increasing mobility difficulty. She had seen on the horizon trains passing along. Looking at the tiny limited map in the guide book it was clear a railway line ran through Sahagun; perhaps there might be a solution here. We had numerous short breaks along the path and a longer one when we got to the little church of the Virgen del Puente just before the outskirts of Sahagun. This was a strange place. The church had clearly been externally renovated – we have no idea if the same was true inside as the church was, inevitably, locked. In the scruffy area in front of the church were both traditional seats and tables, but also futuristic moulded seating banks. There was a huge free-standing arch with recently constructed statues of knights at arms. Clearly it was a place that people congregated at, perhaps for particular feast days. From here the walk into the town was dreary and somewhat ugly. We were walking through an industrial estate when we saw a man who appeared to be a postman delivering mail. He approached us and was excited to discover we were English. He had been learning English through the auspices of a friend who sent him the Times (broadsheet) and the Sun (tabloid) newspapers – we thought this an interesting combination. He was very keen to learn whether or not a particular expression he had learnt was correct: "an apple a day keeps the doctor away" – we wondered which newspaper this was from and why he thought this was such an important phrase - we hoped he would have an opportunity to use it. We asked about trains from Sahagun and he assured us that everyday plenty left from Sahagun to Leon, taking less than an hour to get there. We had found our "keep going" solution.

We arrived at the hostel we had booked into, the Viatoris. This hostel clearly had many private rooms but we were in a huge cavernous dark room and were allocated yet another type of bunk bed. The bunks were in groups of four and despite its being afternoon we had to put on our torches as it was so dark. We were in bottom bunks which were like little metal caves with all sides apart from one being constructed of solid metal. The toilet facilities were communal and ample, but there was nowhere to hang anything so our butcher's hooks came in handy. The real problem with this hostel was the open plan nature of the wash area as the whole place was filled by the stink from some very dodgy sewage system. There must have been sleeping spaces for about fifty people but the place appeared to be half-empty. Someone was already asleep, snoring fit to wake the dead – this turned out to be Hubert whom we had met at Villacazar. All the young Germans and Jenny were here sunning themselves in the back yard. We both went down to the nearby train station and booked tickets for the next day to Leon; we would arrive on Saturday rather than on Sunday as originally planned.

As we were walking down to the station, Charlotte with her walking poles despite the fact that the pack was back at the hostel, we saw along the road side these odd metal posts at regular intervals. They were placed into permanent slots in the roads. It was only when we saw the posters and cottoned on to what the huge round building near the hostel was, that we realised the poles were to hold the barricades used in the running of bulls through the town to the bullring. We had thought this only happened in Pamplona – clearly it happened in other towns too, presumably where there was a bullring. This all felt very, very Spanish. We stopped in a pleasant road-side café for a drink feeling quite relieved that we had decisively sorted our immediate problem out.

Journal reflection (Jane): We're skipping two sections – just let it go. Henry is an angel; he has booked us in for two more days to the Parador in Leon. Our emergency plan was to stay somewhere cheap and cheerful and just go for the one day to the Parador as already planned, but now we shall be able to truly relax.

That evening we had a pilgrim's menu supper sharing our table with two young men from Kentucky who were practically running the Way. They were getting their packs carried to any old hostel in the town or village they aimed for each day, but they were doing around 40 kilometres a day. Once they got to that place, if there was no room there they collected their packs and moved onto another hostel. Their sole guide was a flyer they had picked up somewhere advertising hostels. We admired their obvious stamina, but as mothers we were concerned for their health – their faces looked dreadful as they were both incredibly sunburnt, with raw red noses and terribly burnt ears. Obviously if one did not wear a sun hat, even the small amount of sun we had experienced could do damage.

Hostel Viatoris at Sahagun

Huge hay stacks frequently seen along the Meseta.

This path next to the road is called the Senda, or the Peregrinos' Autopista.

Charlotte applying anti-inflammatory gel to her shin splints after the endlessly repetitive plodding along the flat terrain.

Journal reflection (Charlotte): This is a difficult time for me as I feel tearful and worried that I may not be able to complete this wonderful pilgrimage. We have had to use a taxi already when we were beaten by the weather and we had been prepared to take a bus through the suburbs of Leon. However, to miss two whole days of walking and to still not know if resting my shin will help, is extremely upsetting. I feel that the responsibility to sort this out is falling on Jane as I feel so helpless. I feel my body has let me down after walking so far without any problems – I now realise how punishing walking on the Meseta can be. I should not have been so over-confident. I do so hope the rest period will help.

Days 24-26. May 25 – 27 Sahagun – Leon (forced rest period)

Despite the smell emanating from the toilets, we slept reasonably well and stopped for breakfast at the same café we took coffee at the day before. At the station we got talking to other pilgrims also waiting for the train to Leon. There was a chap from Canada who taught at a Mormon university and was going for a rest period to Leon and a young woman who had only intended to do a short part of the Way before starting a Spanish language course. On the train itself there were clearly other pilgrims; whether they were taking a break like us or finishing a stage was not clear. In a bare 45 minutes we travelled from Sahagun to Leon, a distance that would have taken us two days to walk in our original schedule.

There was a fifteen minute slow walk from the station to the hotel where we left our rucksacks with the concierge and went out to find the city centre. This was probably a mistake for Charlotte, but we were too early to access our room. We found a bookshop selling some books in English and bought one each to see us through the next couple of days. We sat for a long time at a pavement café where we chatted with a husband and wife. He had done the Camino Way the previous year and wanted to show his wife where he had been. She said the pilgrimage seemed to have profoundly affected her husband and had we found likewise? Well, we had to confess that we were mostly pre-occupied each day with where to sleep, what to eat, which bits of laundry to do, what provisions to purchase for the next day, where to find an open shop and how to find the next toilet – profundity tended to get pushed off the agenda. Leon was far busier than Burgos and had a much more metropolitan feel to it. We returned to the hotel to finally get access to our room, which was utterly delightful. After bathing, laundry and having lunch we did some catch-up blogging. The following blog extracts give a diverse impression of what we have been experiencing to-date.

Blog (Jane) Saturday, 25 May 2013 Not an Ensalada Mixta

(To explain the title; every pilgrim menu has, either as a choice or a compulsory dish, a mixed salad. It can be a bit repetitive. Here it acts as a metaphor for odds and sods – a mixture, not of salad, but other sundries.)

We have already shown you some pictures of funny things we have seen, but here we want to share a few interesting and/or strange things we have encountered.

The other day we were happily walking through North West Spain when all of a sudden we were transported to The Shire. People told us these are used by the locals to store their wine in. However, as you can see there are a number of chimneys and TV aerials. Anyway, how could the one little old lady who is the only resident in all these Spanish villages ever drink that amount of wine?! So -- must be Hobbits -- or returning Pilgrims as apparently one´s feet become very broad and hobbit-like after walking the Camino.

As you all know we are walking through Spain. A hot country. You think the weather is unseasonal in the UK but you are not walking here at 07.30 yesterday morning. As we set out we saw all around us drooping flowers and frost-rimed leaves. By mid-day we were slapping on the suntan lotion.

Frosted leaves

Lots of people say how nice it must be walking with your sister. I am not sure Charlotte entirely concurs with this sentiment as at every opportunity she makes a new friend.

This was us a few days ago at Boadillo chilling out (chilling being the operative word – we barely have these fleeces off our backs).

Now a little update on how and where we are. Have we mentioned the concept of the Tourigrino to you? These are Peregrinos who get all their kit transferred from place to place and dash past us with a bounce in their step carrying miniscule day packs. Well -- we have sort of, temporarily become tourigrinos. Yesterday Charlotte's shin splints (they call it tendonitis here) became quite severe and she could barely hobble along. As the Camino Way always provides, luck would have it that we had hobbled into the only place with a major railway station -- no brainer- we caught the train to Leon today so Charlotte can get three days without any walking and hopefully we can be back on the road on Tuesday. Unfortunately we are having to stay in the Leon Parador (google it or watch Martin Sheen's "The Way"). We are quite chilled (that's the G&T) and philosophical (that's the hot baths and huge fluffy towels) about this enforced interruption to our pilgrimage. We may even have to get Charlotte's pack transported for a couple of days. However, given the mega dosage in each tablet purchased in the pharmacies here, Charlotte shouldn't feel the sharp stick I shall be poking her with.

Blog (Charlotte) Sunday, 26 May 2013 rest day at Leon Culture Vultures

Here we are in Spain, a Catholic country so we have of course been surrounded at times by ruins and ancient ecclesiastical buildings. So we thought we would take the opportunity to visit some as we passed through pueblos, towns and cities. We have spent hours walking around and then around and even around again admiring the architecture, stature, grandeur, stonework, carvings and gargoyles - all from the outside as they are always flipping closed!!!! We have managed in total to get into four churches, two Cathedrals which are public museums and two proper churches in small towns, one of which was only open as a wedding party were about to arrive. Once we did manage to get in we had to grope about in the pitch dark to find the offertory candles to light and then use the meagre flame to find the box for the donation. We went to a pilgrim mass at Granon where the lights were lit as the service began to reveal Spain's gold reserves. Blingtastic! We have been told that the churches are all locked because of said bling, but it does seem strange on a pilgrim route. What is evident are the riches the Camino Way has brought to the Church over the centuries as even the smallest hamlet has an enormous church, and we mean enormous.

Here you can see part of an ancient facade on the outside of what was an enormous church which was of course closed. Take note of what happens to sinful people!

154

Part of the Rococo section in the enormous Burgos cathedral, Charlotte spent so long looking up, that the next day she was dizzy from either a trapped nerve or a surfeit of piety!

This was a ruin of a convent where in the past bread was left in special alcoves for passing pilgrims

Yippee, an open door.

This beautiful church was dedicated to the Virgin of the Bridge and was in the middle of nowhere, (just outside Sahagun) beautifully restored but locked.

Leon cathedral is an enormous Gothic edifice, renowned for its beautiful stained glass windows. Jane looked round this as I rested my leg. It involved the largest restoration of a medieval cathedral anywhere in the world as its light and airy construction made it vulnerable to collapse.

An extremely pretty little Church just on the Spanish side of the Pyrenees. It looks from the picture as if we got inside. Don't you believe it. Jane had to stick her camera through a hole in the door.

We have met a few Virgins along the way. They are often enclosed in glass cases and quite hard to take a good picture of. This one was a rather special one in Azofra located near a small park that had been constructed for pilgrims to rest awhile in. Jane and I were actually having a bit of a laugh as the Christ Child looked not unlike a ventriloquist's dummy with enormous feet facing the wrong way. At this point an old chap approached speaking ten to the dozen in Spanish. He was very pleased we were taking such an interest and from what we could gather this Virgin is the patroness of La Rioja. Maybe that explains the sculptor's idiosyncratic modelling! What do you think?

On a less spiritual note, we have been so impressed by the investment in every village, small town and, of course city, in state-of-the-art play equipment and exercise machines for children and youngsters. However, in the more than 250 miles we have travelled so far and at whatever time of day we pass by, we have yet to see a child in a park. Actually we have yet to see a child outside of the city. We suspect that the Pied Piper is not German but is in fact Spanish and alive and well clacking his castanets -- maybe we'll meet the kids in the Leon hills.

There are lots of children in the cities. Coincidentally we tend to get to cities at weekends and every Saturday and Sunday little boys get dressed up in white military suits and little girls put on long white frocks and First Holy Communions take place. This is followed by the FHC party (bit like American Bar Mitzvah do's - or so it seems. The whole family is dressed up to the nines).

In terms of the Spanish language we are trying our best with our two phrase books. There are certain phrases and words that one quickly masters, for example "dos cafe con leche por favor", "vino tinto para mi" (Charlotte), " un vaso di agua para mi" (Jane). However, there are two words/phrases we constantly are corrected on (must be a dialect thing). Unfortunately they are extremely important words and need to be used every day. We have yet to get them out of our mouths correctly. They are: "cerveza" (Charlotte) and "zumo de naranja" (Jane). We'll keep practising.

On route to Leon

Charlotte arriving at Leon

The stay in Leon was a strange period for us. To optimise the chances of us getting back on the road on Tuesday, we decided that Charlotte would rest up at the hotel, walking minimally – to the computer room or the coffee bar. We did research about shin splints/tendonitis and discovered various ways of strapping the leg to give it support. Charlotte took copious amounts of oral anti-inflammatory (the minimum Spanish dosage was 600mg per tablet rather than the 200mg one gets in British pharmacies) and applied gel several times a day. However, whilst the left shin seemed to be improving, the right shin was not getting better. Jane was worried; Charlotte was tearful. The family back home was secretly making contingency plans. In the meantime Jane went into the city centre, initially as a sight-seer and later as an information gatherer. Her first trip out was to visit the cathedral and buy postcards and stamps. Jane found it a far less intimate city than Burgos. As it was such a big city, she did not see many pilgrims at all, leave alone any she knew. It was a bustling, heaving working city with people going about their working lives. It was a relief to get back to the hotel and have coffee in the bar. The barman at the hotel appeared to take a shine to us, perhaps feeling sympathetic to the predicament we were in. Jane made a second foray out on the Sunday to buy a T-shirt for Charlotte and to make enquiries at the train station about trains to Astorga, in case Charlotte was still not able to walk by Tuesday.

Journal reflection (Jane): This is a difficult time for both of us. Charlotte clearly believes she will have to abandon the pilgrimage as her right shin just will not improve. Consequently she has become extremely (and understandably) emotional. I am trying to find a solution. We cannot stay at this beautiful hotel longer than Monday night, but I am deeply pessimistic that Charlotte will be able to walk. I feel very responsible as I have dragged us both out on this adventure; I have got to make it work for both of us. I am surprising myself, however, by feeling I can let go of convictions about being purist and instead feel comfortable about being pragmatic. If we have to skip another two stages, then we shall.

On getting to the train station that Sunday, Jane discovered it was closed – the American "cowboy" had been right about weekend public transport in Spain. Jane trawled around an enormous outdoor clothes market and found the least-ghastly T-shirt for Charlotte then wandered back to the cathedral square. There she was amazed to discover the tourist information centre was open. Inside, two uniformed women behind the desk were chatting to each other as Jane waited patiently (and then not so patiently) to be served. When she asked about information on trains to Astorga on Tuesday one woman barked at her, "Why do you want a train? What is the matter with the bus?" Having established that there was a bus, Jane asked for details and was told it departed from outside the cathedral. Well, she could see that as this was a pedestrian only area that was unlikely so she asked for a map. The bus station was about 1.5 kilometres from the centre – hardly outside the cathedral. Jane prised the map from the woman's grasp, thanked her and left – the Spanish service sector was a strange beast! The following day Jane went to the bus station to check out how far it was to walk there and to get details of the right bus to catch.

Blog (Jane) Monday, 27 May 2013 third rest day at Leon Parador - Paradise

Well we leave here tomorrow and we shall go by bus to a place called Astorga. From there we shall start walking again on Thursday morning. This will have given Charlotte's shin five days free of serious walking and hopefully she will be able to cope with the mountains of Galicia (aaaghh!).

We have really enjoyed our brief stay here-- well, who wouldn't?! We have of course attempted to retain a serious and contemplative demeanour, but it's hard when you have a glass of wine in your hand and have to nibble at another bowl of olives.

On a practical level we have got our washing done, caught up on BBC world news (anybody want to know the weather in Taiwan?), caught up on sleep, bathed until we look like prunes and re-stocked our wash bags with tiny upmarket shampoos etc. -- just what a pilgrim needs. We are not the only pilgrims doing this. We have met several others either just resting or injured and having an enforced rest -- I know they could have chosen the municipal albergue -- we blame Martin Sheen and the natural hedonism of human kind.

This is the Parador de San Marco, formerly a monastery, school, gaol, stable, military headquarters and nearly demolished in the 19th century -- thankfully now a lovely hotel and museum.

Charlotte's natural piety shines around her!

We met up with Bethany from Hawaii again at breakfast this morning -- lovely to see her. She is charging ahead as she has a tight deadline.

The bar -- a sort of home-from-home. (Henry did say he was paying!!!!)

The view from our little balcony. (Very private fortunately as our smalls have spent some time drying out here.)

We are now gearing up to get back on The Way -- actually we really can't wait to get going again. More news when we have some.

The other thing that we did before leaving Leon was to find out about the baggage carrying service. We arranged for a company called Jacotrans to collect Charlotte's pack and transport it to Astorga. We were reasonably sure that Charlotte's shin splints had been set off by the persistently uniform walking that the Meseta had allowed and encouraged. We were also reasonably sure that without the additional 20+ pounds on her back Charlotte would manage the walk to and from the bus stations at each end the following day. The baggage carrying service was 7 euros and we thought that, in the circumstance, this was worth it. Jane also booked beds at private hostels all the way through to Sarria to take the strain of uncertainty about accommodation away. Whilst we were still not back in pilgrim mode, we had a sense of moving forward.

Journal reflection (Charlotte): It is wonderful staying in the Parador for three nights. I was in agony yesterday and is so good to rest today. I have texted my friends who have now all replied so I am feeling less lonely. It feels good to have updated our blog and pictures. Jane and Henry are doing all they can to help – they are so sweet and generous. I do not want to let them down. It is good to read others advice on the Confraternity site. I am reassured that I am doing the right thing to heal my leg. This is not how I had imagined the Way would be. It is teaching me not to be too complacent.

Days 27 & 28. May 28th / 29th Leon to Astorga – two more forced rest days (stayed at Astvr Plaza)

The bus from Leon to Astorga took 40 minutes and saved us a two-day walk. Astorga was a large, busy town and when we arrived a big street market was just closing down for the afternoon. It was bitterly cold so we rested in our room, Charlotte putting a flannel from the bathroom in the fridge and then using it as an icepack on her shin. On our second day we ventured a little walking to do some sightseeing. We also met Marcia and Colin from Cornwall in the bar; they and Charlotte got on like a house on fire when they discovered they shared health sector and occupational therapy backgrounds.

Blog (Jane) Wednesday, 29 May 2013 rest day: Howdee Gaudi

Well, sorry to be teaching grandmother to suck eggs as obviously you all know that Antoni Gaudi from Catalan was the father of Catalan modernism and responsible for many architectural masterpieces in Spain, promoting artisanal crafts and skills including ceramics, carpentry, stonemasonry and ironwork to produce his unique style of architecture

This is Gaudi's bishops 'palace in Astorga. You can see he liked a turret. In fact you could be forgiven for thinking we had leaped to Disney Land. It was fascinating inside, however.

These were the amazing vaults inside. Every tile on the edges was hand crafted.

I don't know whether you have a taste for decorative flying ducks across your living room wall, but clearly in 13th century the penchant was for flying bishops.

There were an amazing number of very ancient, but very exquisite figures of the Virgin Mary. She was often missing her crown and the fruit (??) she was holding in her right hand. She would always be dressed in the rich raiment of the period and decorated in gold leaf. The figure above is a particularly nice example from the medieval period.

We also visited the cathedral and its museum and we were amazed at the work that went into embroidering the church vestments -- gold and metallic threads cannot have been easy to manipulate and the curly fleeces on the Lamb of God must have taken weeks to complete and nobody would have seen this detail.

Here Jane is hanging onto a pilgrim's staff to avoid being blown into the Hills of Leon (which we face tomorrow).

Charlotte is at the entrance to a peaceful little park.

Astorga is both a popular pilgrim town, with many pilgrims passing through all day, but also other tourists are here - we guess they are visiting the chocolate museum and purchasing bars of chocolate the size of gold ingots on display in the numerous sweet shops on every street.

Blog (Charlotte): From the park we had wonderful views of the mountains in the distance; we head off tomorrow towards them. I am very hopeful my leg will be OK; we have rested and I am taking massive anti-inflammatory tablets, icing my shin, rubbing in embrocation and strapping it. (We watched very helpful You Tube films to instruct on appropriate strapping) We have also been walking around Astorga and going up and down many steps. My leg is sore but 90% better. So as long as we rest frequently and take each day as it comes we will get to Santiago in about 12 days!!!!

A new pack needed for all Charlotte's shin splint-related pharmaceuticals!

Resting for an additional two days at Astorga had been absolutely the right decision to make. We also decided to continue with the Jacotrans service for the foreseeable future so as to optimise conditions for a successful continuation of the pilgrimage. It was at this point that we picked up a comment on the blog from our brother Mark. We discovered that Jane's son, Matthew, had been arranging with his Dad that he would come over to Spain to walk each day with his Mum whilst ensuring Charlotte caught an appropriate bus until such time as she was completely better. Henry could not come over as he was committed to looking after grandchildren and his elderly mother. It was such a kind idea but fortunately we did not have to disrupt his life as we cautiously but confidently stepped out that Thursday morning and got back on the road again.

Leaving Astorga after our five-day forced rest break.

CHAPTER EIGHT   ON THE ROAD AGAIN

Day 29. May 30th Astorga – Rabanal del Camino 21.4K/13.4M (stayed at NS de Pilar)

Today, Thursday, we set off on the pilgrim's road again; it was absolutely brilliant! We had almost 13.5 miles of gradual climb to do as we were approaching the Montes de Leon, which would be highest point of the pilgrimage. We were already very high so in terms of actual climb it would not be as big as the Pyrenees behind us or O'Cebreiro ahead of us, but it was a reasonably challenging day given it was the first day back after our enforced rest period. We left at 08.00 in the morning and did not arrive at our destination of Rabenal del Camino until 15.45 in the afternoon as we walked slowly and rested often. We met a lovely Jewish couple at a café, Jacob and Ella – both seasoned treckers. Jacob had made customised umbrella-walking poles for them both – very interesting. It had been incredibly cold whilst we had been in Astorga and the wind blew fiercely. This day, in contrast was bright and cold with a little less wind. For the following six days we were unable to access a computer so we include here part of the blog we eventually wrote much later.

Blog (Jane) Tuesday, 4 June 2013)

We're On The Road Again, We're On The Road Again

Well we're back - back walking, back blogging. Actually we have been back walking for six days now but haven't been able to access a computer -- I know - it's Spain! It has been absolutely brilliant to be walking again and everyday Charlotte's shin gets stronger and stronger. It is not quite right yet, so we are having Charlotte's backpack (with loads of my stuff in as well) portered by a firm called Jacotrans (brilliant business to be in). Charlotte keeps thinking she has left a baby somewhere and we are having to accept we have become "tourigrinos".

Last time we blogged we were a pair of culture-vultures resting in Astorga. Since then we have done a bit of walking. We left Astorga bright and early thanks, not to Charlotte's usual phone alarm, but to the extremely useful "character clock" immediately outside our window. This clock very usefully struck every quarter of the hour and of course on the hour, (the appropriate number of bongs) and just in case you hadn´t heard it the first time, it repeated itself just after the hour. We woke up on time.

First he hit it then she did. (I took this photo from our Velux window.)

During our rest period we had seen pilgrims coming into town wearing every garment they possessed and with cagoules zipped up to their noses. We had read and heard about the terrible weather we would be likely to meet in the Montes de Leon that we had to climb over. The guide book (our bible) talked of the almost perpetual shroud of mist. Anyway, as you can see from the photos below, we had a little more luck than that.

Blue sky, sunshine and no pack was the order of the day. We went cautiously but the day went brilliantly.

Poor old us, forced to look at this view. There were snow-capped mountains in all directions. This is an indicator of the temperature. This day and for every day since we have been accompanied by the sound of cuckoos and skylarks and the scent of broom (which is white here) and heather (which is head-high and shades of deep pink) -- a heady mix.

Stopping for a restorative coffee en route to Rabanal.

This is a picture for all the "doubting Thomases" who didn't believe I had seen a huge green lizard as big as a small kitten back when we saw the huge moth. (They are very hard to photograph as they are well camouflaged and don't stand still).

This is the Pilgrims Oak Tree. We were very tired but nearly at our destination and very pleased with our progress.

The room we had booked at the hostel was lovely; a separate room with a very clean shared bathroom. We got some ice from the bar at the hostel for a pack for Charlotte's shin. Her leg was swollen and made a strange grinding noise, but was less painful than it had been. We went out to find somewhere to eat that evening and passed a man with an eagle on his arm. Sometimes it is a real shame not to have enough Spanish to ask the simple question – why? One of the most curious sights we had seen that day was when we were passing through one of the many dilapidated villages, where half the houses are in ruins and one is being rebuilt. As we walked we saw a large windowless barn. Part way up was a hole in the wall across which had been nailed some Perspex. Behind this makeshift window was a small basket of large cats. Was the "window" there so the cats could see out, or was it there so pilgrims could admire the cats? Whatever the answer, it showed a caring nature on the part of someone.

Day 30. May 31st Rabanal del Camino – Riego de Ambros 20.8K/13M (stayed at Riego de Ambros)

This was the big climb up to the significant landmark of La Cruz de Ferro standing at 1,505 metres (4,890 feet). In fact it was a reasonably gentle and gradual climb in the most glorious bright, cool and breezy weather – possibly the nicest walking day of the whole pilgrimage.

Continuation of blog not posted until 4th June: Jane –

This day the sun shone again and once more it was pretty cold. We were heading for the highest point of the whole Camino Way -- yes higher than the Pyrenees! An indication of how clean the air was, was this group of furry" trees. This lichen was incredibly long and soft, a little like seaweed. (See next picture)

As you can see it's cold but beautiful with lavender and heather and mountains and blue sky -- OK we'll stop rubbing it in -- some of you are still working.

This is La Cruz de Ferro - an important stage of the Camino Way where people are encouraged to let go of troubles/sorrows they may have. There is a small mountain (see second photo) of tokens and mementoes that have been left by the thousands of pilgrims that pass by. Here you see Charlotte is leaving her own token and, if she felt light before without her backpack she virtually floated the rest of the way down this mountain!

Henry said this is the nearest I would get to heaven (what does he know?)

As you can see the sky is gloriously clear. However, we later met a German woman, Claudia, who had gone up and over just the day before and it snowed while she was crossing -- she saw nothing - nada. On the other hand this is what we saw!

Journal reflection (Jane): There were quite a few pilgrims congregated at La Cruz de Ferro. Some were quite emotional as great store is set on the importance of this place. Charlotte left one of the three holy medals she had brought with her on the pilgrimage, but I had chosen to bring nothing. I thought I might regret this, but in the event I found the place rather tatty and I was very conscious of not wanting to be "pilgrimy" for the sake of it. One chap was in tears for his departed wife; but for me it was just a pile of stones. In contrast, I had been deeply moved at a little non-descript shrine part way up the Alto del Perdon – but not here.

Journal reflection (Charlotte): I left my First Holy Communion medal tucked into a band on the pole at the top of this small mountain of stones and tokens. I felt very emotional at this letting go of the dreadful Catholic guilt that has caused me such grief in my life – it felt very cathartic.

That evening we had dinner at a hostel/bar on the outskirts of the village. We met Jacob and Ella again, who were staying in the same place as us. We had met up a few times over the past couple of days. Jacob was very emphatic that he was not a "religious Jew" but was doing the Camino Way because it was "do-able" – they had trekked in Nepal and other distant places, but now, in retirement were enjoying themselves doing more manageable walks. We had first met when he was buying a slice of the deepest tortilla we had seen. Most tortillas are flattish, like a thick omelette. This one, however, was as deep as a three-sponge layer cake – it was enormous. The proprietor told Ella how it was made; a slow cook methodology requiring some special utensils – we never saw another tortilla like it. We also talked about a Portuguese man and his wife and dog we had both seen the day before – they were difficult to miss. They had walked to Santiago de Compostela from their home in Portugal because he had been made redundant. They were walking to Jerusalem and when we met them they were walking against the flow on the way up to La Cruz de Ferro. Both the wife and the dog looked glum; the husband looked exhausted. He was pushing (not pulling) a handcart with their possessions in along this rutted, stony uphill track – it appeared to be madness. He was surely going to kill himself.

At the restaurant there was a young Brazilian, Victor, engaged in conversation with a very loud German woman. At first we thought they must know one another as she was talking about the death of the young man's mother or sister and how he must find the pilgrimage a solace and find peace in what he was doing. After a bit he excused himself and the woman then latched on to Jacob and Ella. She clearly wanted to talk about the spiritual wonders of walking the Camino Way and how transforming it must be. Jacob would have none of it – in his opinion people walked the Camino Way because it was so easy to do: there were hostels and bars all along the route and if one wanted one could stay in hotels much of the time and get one's baggage taken from place to place. To a large extent he had a good point, but we rather thought he was going to argue black was white and white was black just because the woman was so irritatingly opinionated. Clearly the Camino Frances is "do-able" and very well supported; it is a vital part of the local economy along the route. However, it is still difficult – although that is obviously a relative term.

The following day we had breakfast at the pension and helped translate for some Americans as the Spanish host was a French speaker. The small bit of French and Italian Jane has learnt has proved surprisingly useful on this journey. Some Spanish would have proved even more useful. This had been a lovely place to stay with the most spectacular views of snow-topped mountains from the balcony outside our room. The proprietor had given us an icepack for Charlotte's shin, which had stood up to the climb well and was improving slowly. The only slight quibble we had was with the absolutely tiny en suite shower room that had been built in the corner of the fairly small bedroom. One had to sit on the toilet sideways as one's knees would not fit in sitting normally and as for getting in and out of the shower ... In addition it only had three-quarter length partition walls that stopped well below the ceiling, so it is just as well we were two sisters and not two friends a little squeamish about bodily functions. (No, we are not fixated – but going on this type of pilgrimage is a bit like a sort of extended camping holiday and all these creature comforts – or dis-comforts – are noticed.) We would be far less inclined to take our lives at home for granted in the future.

Day 31. June 1st Riego de Ambros – Fuente Cacabelos 27.1K/16.9M (stayed at Hostal Santa Maria)

Today was a taxing day. It was going to be over 27 kilometres (nearly17 miles) long. The first stage was lovely: deep valleys, beautiful streams running down the valleys, stony descents that required care. As we walked through the pretty town of Molinaseca, we saw Hubert sitting at a bus stop. His blisters were still causing him difficulties so he was going to get the bus for the four kilometres into Ponferrada. To reduce the long mileage that day and after the strain-on-the-shins descent, we decided to join him. We met his new German friend, Claudia (who had been up in the snow on La Cruz de Ferro the day before us). We were to be enormously grateful that we took this short bus hop as we got incredibly lost in Ponferrada and ended up adding significantly to our distance by walking in entirely the wrong direction for a mile and a half then having to re-trace our steps before eventually finding the pilgrim signs.

It was a very warm day. We had come down from the cold heights and the temperature was much warmer. We were not really surprised to discover that it was far more exhausting walking in the warmth than in the cold. The plod out of Ponferrada was interminable, with new road ways and roundabouts with no signs making the going more difficulty. We came across a young woman looking very lost and grateful to have company to walk with. Meg, from New Jersey, was doing two weeks of the Camino Way as part of her post-graduate studies at a university in London. She had developed a terrible, painful rash on her legs from her walking socks and was going slowly. We were a little concerned about her but later, when we met Vicky from Zimbabwe, we left the two young women to walk together.

Today we passed many very tidy, well-maintained market gardens. We wondered whether their owners belonged to co-operatives and sold their produce through their co-op or whether they just took them to market themselves. Each "garden" was about four times the size of the usual allotment back home, so clearly the produce was not intended just to feed the family. It all gave a very neat, industrious and small-scale feeling to this part of Spain after the vast tracts of farmed land on the Meseta. This day's walk took us nine hours- we did not get to our destination in Cacabelos until 17.10. We were both exhausted and Jane was very headachy.

We had a lovely room with a proper bath, so after the delights of a soak and having done the laundry we went out to eat somewhere. The first place we tried was hosting a stag do. The groom was dressed as a faux toreador but wearing tights, with an enormous toy cockerel placed in a prominent and explicit position. Everyone else had shrill party-type whistles. We had to move on.

Blog posted later but relevant extract included here (Jane):

This day we climbed down out of the mountains and met the Spanish heat for

181

almost the first time. It was also a very long day's walk. We got lost in Ponferrada and felt very hot and frazzled. However, we met a lovely American girl, Meg, from New Jersey but studying in London and doing the Camino Way as part of her practical research into the interface of tourism and religion. She suggested the interesting picture we took outside a little church might be a depiction of the four houses of Hogwarts.

Sometime later we met Vicky from Zimbabwe. Both Vicky and Meg were suffering with leg injuries. Meg is flying home on the same flight as us so we will hopefully meet her again.

Charlotte's shin was getting so much better, but Jane's headaches were beginning to play up. However, we both hoped that the following day we would be able to take the scenic route described in the guide book rather than the road route, even though this would mean a significant climb.

Day 32. June 2nd Fuente Cacabelos – Trabadelo 21.1K/13.3M (stayed at El Puente Peregrino)

This day was a day for the senses: seeing the beauty of gorges, vineyards, chestnut orchards and swallow tail butterflies; smelling the delicious scents of pine woods; tasting the oh-so-refreshing freshly-squeezed orange that many bars sell; feeling the effort of climbing up hills and feeling the need for more water than we had with us;

hearing the braying of a lonely donkey and the scuttle of many big brown lizards. It was not a day for walking with or bumping into many pilgrims and because of this our senses were probably even more alive to the sensations around us.

We were still walking through the province of Castille y Leon and we had experienced such very different scenery within the one province. We had passed through towns, cities, dilapidated pueblos and picture-postcard villages. Only a little while before this day we had been walking through the beautiful but very flat Meseta. We had then climbed the hills again and seen the snow-capped peaks. We had descended to the heat and busyness of the old city of Ponferrada and this day we were walking through gorges, past vineyards and we were climbing hills. It was not just the scenery that had been varied, it was also the weather: fine, but changeable and cold; rainy, snowy, muddy and cold; bright, windy and cold; sunny and cold; and, finally, sunny and hot. We would shortly be saying goodbye to this enormous but very versatile province. After this day, there would be just one more day of walking in Castille y Leon.

We were out walking by 07.20. The countryside around us was full of vineyards but surrounded by hills; the mist lay in the valleys beneath us whilst we walked in the morning sun. We stopped for breakfast and we stopped for fresh orange juice; stupidly we did not stop to top up our water bottles. After 10.5 kilometres when we reached a little town, Villafranca del Bierzo, we would have to make the decision whether or not to stay on the track next to the highway or to climb nearly 400 metres (1,300 ft.) up and go over the Alto Pradela. Dear Reader, you may find it bizarre, but we chose the up-and-over route as it was going to knock the road route into a cocked hat as far as scenery was concerned; we were booked in to accommodation at Trabadelo so it would not matter if we took ages to do the walk.

Just before we began the ascent we bumped into Victor, the young Brazilian man who had hurt his knee whom we had seen at Riego de Ambros two days before. He was clearly dithering over whether to take the "high road" or not. We felt a little guilty as we thought we might have forced his decision: two women considerably older than him saying they were going to do the climb as it would be far prettier on the top route – how does a young man say – well I'm going on the easy path? In fact after the first half mile or so we did not see Victor until we arrived at Trabadelo where we found him tucking into some food, clearly having got there way ahead of us.

The path we took went up and up, then it went up and up again. Every time we thought we had got most of the climb done, we would turn a corner and discover more hill to go up. The first leg of the route was part of a larger local walk and had recently had the hedge rows cut back so wild flower debris was strewn everywhere. After a while this route turned off and the Camino Way went in a different direction. The usual arrows were there to guide us, but they were very few and far between and sometimes the path to take was almost indiscernible, particularly after the chestnut groves just beyond the summit. We got splendid distant views at the top and could see far below the "easy route" winding below next to a major road and passing beneath a motorway high up on stilts. We could see the scars on the hillsides where forest had been harvested. We sat in the chestnut grove to rest and saw lizards and butterflies – it was lovely. Our big problem was we had to ration our water as foolishly we had not topped our bottles up before we began the ascent. This scenic route was nearly 11 kilometres and it was a warm day. We could have done with twice as much water as we had.

The descent presented some of the usual challenges of walking down steep hills together with the added conundrum of the signs seeming to disappear; we had to use our common sense and follow our noses and we were mindful that this had not always been an effective methodology earlier in the pilgrimage. Fortunately this day it worked, but once again we realised that coming down was as hard as climbing up – just in a different way.

Trabadelo was a long thin village strung along the road that would lead us the following day to our last very big climb, up to O'Cebreiro. After walking in the wrong direction up the village, talking to Victor for a bit, we walked back and found our lodgings for the night – run by a Dutch woman and her Spanish husband. They were lovely people and gave us an ice for a pack for Charlotte's leg but also pointed out they sold an "ice bandage" that could be applied many times and remained cold – too good to be true – we bought one (it was to prove invaluable later in the journey). Our room was lovely and the shared bathroom was clean. After bathing, some laundry, resting and icing the leg we went for drinks.

Now for most of the pilgrimage we two had been sharing the challenge of speaking Spanish in bars and cafes. We were equally bad at pronouncing the Spanish for beer and for orange juice – to be fair to us the pronunciation did seem to vary from province to province. Jane had done all the phone bookings to hostels and to the baggage carrying firm over the past few days and had got a very few phrases off pat – she could not yet spell her name using the Spanish alphabet, however. This day we went to a bar where Charlotte had to draw not only on her small Spanish lexicon but also on her much broader repertoire of mime. We had bumped into Hubert and Claudia and were about to have a drink with them outside a bar on the pavement. All of a sudden Jane began to cough and this rapidly became a choking gasping for breath – possibly as a consequence of too little to drink all day. Charlotte sprung into action. Galloping into the bar she asked for a "un vaso de agua para mi hermana por favour" adding "pronto" for good measure; then - "quickly, as she is choking; she cannot breathe; she cannot catch her breath." – that bit was delivered entirely through mime. She got the water. Thank goodness for Rose Bruford's Saturday morning drama club way back in childhood!

Blog posted later but relevant extract included here (Jane):

It was another gorgeous day and started with a steep gorge –

Jane in gorge.

After going down, of course we then had to go up a very, very big hill. We could have stayed on the road, but this was a much more beautiful option. Apart from Victor from Brazil in front of us it seemed as if we were the only pilgrims taking the high road. We walked down through mature sweet chestnut groves -- no pictures as by this time we were exhausted and somewhat dehydrated -- not used to walking in such heat. Arrived eventually at a lovely "gastro pub" run by a Dutch woman and her Spanish partner.

An example of the very varied countryside we travelled through.

The place we stayed at described itself as a gastro pub and in fact the food that evening was delicious. The owner very kindly agreed to let Jane have white wine as part of the pilgrim menu instead of the usual red as red wine precipitated serious migraines. He was the first and only person to do this.

Day 33. June 3rd Trabadelo – O'Cebreiro 18.4K/11.5M (stayed at Venta Celta)

Despite having a comfortable room, Jane slept badly and felt rotten as the day started. We were out walking by 06.40 into a cold morning. We walked in silence for the first hour until we found somewhere for coffee and toast and this produced a civilising influence on us. We were making extremely good progress and were just beginning to think that this final big climb was going to be a doddle. Little did we realise we were very much in the foothills.

Blog written later but extract included her (Jane): *Today (Monday June 3rd) was a big day for us. We had to climb O'Cebreiro, as tall as Ben Nevis. We set off at 06.40 and fairly galloped the first six miles. We then positively crawled the remainder of the way. It was another stunning day so it was good to set off early and get the climb over before the heat of the day. We were so ahead of ourselves we arrived at 12.50 before the pack had arrived and in plenty of time to become "Ladies who Lunch" -- and we did. We also became tourists and bought pins for our hats and Galician music CDs (I bet you can't wait!)*

Up, up and away she goes (yeh -- where´s the pack!!)

Ah there´s the pack -- no wonder Jane is stopping for (yet another) breather.

This was a momentous moment for us. We have to travel through four provinces in Spain: Navarre, Rioja, Castille y Leon and finally Galicia. Now we are on the homeward stretch!

Jane relaxing in O'Cebreiro

We both found the climb up O'Cebreiro far harder than we had anticipated. (925 metres of elevation from Trabadelo – 3,034 feet.) Clearly Charlotte was still nursing a recovering leg whilst Jane was dealing with her recurrent headaches and a very painful shoulder. However, it was more than that; we were not as fit as we had hoped and expected that we would be by this stage of the walk. We stopped twice at bars for something to drink and to rest. We met a delightful couple who had cycled from Lourdes in Southern France and were now taking their bikes on this mountain route to Santiago. They were so complimentary of us having walked from St Jean Pied de Port, calling us "heroes", that it helped us feel a little less wrecked.

At one point towards the last third of the climb, in order to avoid a long downhill stretch after having climbed so high, we stayed on the road and did not divert onto the signed track. The gain was: not having to descend and then having to win back that height again; the loss was: we ended up walking further. As we approached the last part of the climb on a stony track that zig-zagged upwards, Jane was staggering along in exhaustion. It was such a relief to get to the top and then to find our room for the night.

O'Cebreiro may be a bit of a "Marmite" village – one either loved or hated it. We thought it was charming. Yes, it was commercial and prettily renovated in an authentic Galician manner, but it was friendly and a welcome change from dilapidated and deserted villages. Clearly the village was a tourist day-trip destination with many tourists coming up from the Galician side by bus, car and even on horseback. There were clearly firms that hired horses with guides so people could ride up O'Cebreiro from either Galicia or Castille y Leon. We had seen one such guide taking his horses back down the mountain as we had been climbing up.

We decided to bathe and then eat lunch at a bar rather than eating in the evening. We discovered that we had moved into the province of pulpo (octopus) – everybody was eating it and Charlotte decided that once we got to Sarria in a couple of days' time, she too would have some. Jane was entirely happy not to go native with that sort of thing. We enjoyed wandering around and noseying around the gift shops. We sat and took in the view – hills in every direction and we marvelled at the splendid weather – the area could be very misty and rainy.

We visited the little church in the village and gave our thanks to the man who had invented the yellow arrow system of Camino Way signage who is buried there. Whilst no longer being a practising

Catholic, Jane found the pilgrim's prayer (attributed to Fray Dino of La Faba) enlarged on huge boards, interesting. Only the final part relates to Christianity and one can translate that in any way one chooses. It was really about using the experiences that build you to influence your life to the good. It is reproduced below:

Prayer of La Faba

"Although I may have travelled all the roads,

Crossed mountains and valleys from East to West,

If I have not discovered the freedom to be myself,

I have arrived nowhere.

Although I may have shared all of my possessions

With people of other languages and cultures;

Made friends with Pilgrims of a thousand paths,

Or shared albergue with saints and princes,

If I am not capable of forgiving my neighbour tomorrow,

I have arrived nowhere.

Although I may have carried my pack from beginning to end

And waited for every Pilgrim in need of encouragement,

Or given my bed to one who arrived later than I,

Given my bottle of water in exchange for nothing;

If upon returning to my home and work,

I am not able to create brotherhood

Or to make happiness, peace and unity,

I have arrived nowhere.

Although I may have had food and water each day,

And enjoyed a roof and shower every night;

Or may have had injuries well attended,

If I have not discovered in all that the love of God,

I have arrived nowhere.

Although I may have seen all the monuments

And contemplated the best sunsets;

Although I may have learned a greeting in every language;

Or tried the clean water from every fountain;

If I have not discovered who is the author

Of so much free beauty and so much peace,

I have arrived nowhere.

If from today I do not continue walking on your path,

Searching for and living according to what I have learned;

If from today I do not see in every person, friend or foe

A companion on the Camino;

If from today I cannot recognise God,

The God of Jesus of Nazareth

As the one God of my life,

I have arrived nowhere."

We felt very satisfied with ourselves. We had walked across three of the four provinces and now had around seven days of walking left. We had climbed the biggest mountains and largely conquered the Meseta. We had resolved Charlotte's injury problem and we had not let our other annoying ailments impede us unduly. We had no idea what Galicia was going to be like, except we had read it was a very wet and rainy province. We were looking forward to this final stage of the adventure.

Blog continued (Jane): *First picture is the view from our window. We felt as if we were on top of the world, both physically and metaphorically. Second picture is the same view but at 06.00 this morning (June 4th) showing the mist in the valleys and the mountain tops floating on seas of cloud.*

Journal reflection (Jane): The beginning and end of this day have been such a contrast. I woke after such a bad night's sleep at Trabadelo, feeling ill with a terrible head and fearful that I could not cope with the climb today. Yesterday's climb had taken a toll on me that I had not expected; I thought I would be fitter and stronger than in fact I am. Charlotte and I had words because I was bad-tempered and hurt her feelings. We both set off in a sulk, but walking does knock such silliness out of you after a bit. My shoulder was becoming very painful which compounded my anxieties about managing the climb. It was such hard work, but we did it. I had read much about how pilgrims leap up O'Cebreiro like gazelles having honed themselves through the earlier stages of the pilgrimage and I was disappointed that I felt so wrecked. After an hour or so we had settled into our usual walking routine and all was fine between us, which was good as we need to support each other. By the end of the day we were elated with our achievement and while the day had a bad start it had a mellow finish.

Journal reflection (Charlotte): Started the day feeling out of sorts with Jane, but ended the day in gentle harmony. It was a strenuous but wonderful day of walking. It is amazing to be in Galicia now and even the temperature is warm!

CHAPTER NINE   GLORIOUS GALICIA

Day 34. June 4th O'Cebreiro – Triacastela   21.3K/13.3M (stayed at Complexo Xacbeo)

Below, on the next page, you can see a picture of the place we stayed at the night after O'Cebreiro. You can immediately see what we have been doing with the packs. On the left of the picture is Charlotte's pack; Jane's is on the right. Since Leon we had been getting Charlotte's pack picked up by Jacotrans and taken to our next hostel. Jane phoned them up, put the 7 euros in the little brown envelope, put our names on and the hostel it was to go to and left the pack at whatever the current hostel's collection point was. We had to change the service provider towards the end of the trip and the cost came down from seven to three euros (competition, we guessed as there are even more pilgrims just walking the final 100 kilometres). We were a little anxious at first about whether the pack would be picked up and whether it would arrive at the correct place; but it always did, with a new brown envelope for the following day. We never had the money stolen as we had been warned did sometimes happen. Anyway, to optimise on our 7 euro outlay, we crammed into Charlotte's pack as much as we could from Jane's – her sleeping bag, spare clothes and wash stuff. This is where the huge expanding "collar" on our Gregory ladies 45/55 litre sacks came into its own. In the picture, Charlotte's pack is at its utmost stretch – a position we empathised with! Jane's pack was, consequently much lighter than it had been, possibly from 22 lbs down to 15lbs.

We had 155 kilometres still to walk (96 miles). It would take us two days to walk to Sarria, then around four days for the final 100 (approximately) kilometres into Santiago de Compostela. We loved Galicia; not just because it was the last leg of a long adventure, but because it was beautiful. We immediately appreciated the "intimacy" of Galicia. We were surrounded by mountains and rolling hills as we descended that morning from O'Cebreiro, but we also quickly saw small scale husbandry and small scale fields. The patchwork fields were very reminiscent of England. We had read that much of the farming was done by women as often the men had gone to seek work in the cities. We cannot say how true that is, but we certainly saw women driving tractors, taking water to livestock and gathering in barrows full of vegetables. We came across our favourite pilgrim statue quite early on that day. The statue was very tall and set on a high promontory at Alto San Roque. He was leaning into the wind and holding onto his hat.

We had one short but steep climb down and climb up – but as they say, "the Way will provide" – at the end of the climb was a bar selling the most delicious freshly squeezed orange juice. There were a group of lively and vibrant young Americans there having some refreshment. We later saw them several more times: walking along as a group saying the rosary out loud, being ultra-fussy in the restaurant attached to the hostel that night and very kindly looking after each other when one of the group hurt her knee coming out of Sarria. Instinctively we had been a bit wary of people being ostentatiously religious on the pilgrimage. In fact people wore their beliefs very lightly and privately on the whole. We had shared a hostel a couple of times with some young American fundamentalist Christians. They had both amused and irritated us. They spent a lot of time working on a web site to "sell" their evangelical ideas. They were determined to go to such countries as India to teach people there their business management methodologies and to convert them. Well – one should never judge a book by its cover but … They looked all of around 20 years old, very nerdy and one could not help but think that they would be advised to learn some business techniques from India rather than thinking they were able to impart anything useful; and as for converting the Buddhists, Hindus, Jains, Sikhs and Muslims to Christianity .. …well!

We had left O'Cebreiro at 07.05 and arrived at Triacastela at 13.45. So we had taken a fair old time to cover just over 13 miles. We were staying in the hostel, Complexo Xacbeo. The local language in Galicia, Galega, is similar to Portuguese, but has some Celtic aspects. We discovered that the "J" we had trouble in pronouncing in the other regions of Spain was written as an "X" in Galicia –the pronunciation was still problematic and people could still not understand us when we asked for orange juice!

Blog continued (Jane): *As you can see, we are alive and well and enjoying our journey. Charlotte is looking well-pleased as she has just had a near miss with a bowl of tripe -- that will teach her not to learn Spanish before coming to Spain. (Tripe is "callos" in case you're ever in that predicament yourselves.)*

We continue walking for another six days.

We got into the hostel reasonably early. There were very many cyclists at this hostel all with their bikes stored inside. Whilst we have been passed by many cyclists on the Way, we have not yet shared a hostel with any, apart from the French "pirate"; perhaps they have to stay at particular hostels where there is secure housing for their bikes. We were in a large room with only four bunks and one single bed. There were several other rooms elsewhere. It was clean and spacious and, oh joy, there were two pay computers so we could update the blog after a long hiatus. We went for a drink in a bar and then bought a few provisions including a PD James novel for Jane – well, she would have to carry it.

At our hostel we briefly spoke to a chap who was on two hospital-type crutches. He had jumped across a stream awkwardly and had torn a ligament. He had already rested at the hostel for several days and it was clear that he could barely walk. He wanted to complete the pilgrimage, but it looked very doubtful that he would. When we had been faced with our injury conundrum on the day we approached

Sahagun, Jane had remembered the advice given in a particular outdoor magazine she and Henry subscribe to. In this magazine a recent article had taken half a dozen famous climbers and explorers and they each described occasions when they had "turned back". They had been 200 metres from the summit, 100 miles from the South Pole, etc. – very close, but not there. For various reasons, mostly relating to weather and health, they had turned back despite the nearness of the "destination goal" and despite the often huge expense they incurred getting as far as they had. Once, when Jane and Henry had been walking the long-distance route, The Pennine Way, their son, Matthew had joined them for the day. The day involved a lonely walk up high onto Cross Fell, a place reputed to have sun approximately four times a year! The weather on this day was foul: drenching, horizontal and continuous rain together with gale force winds. Matthew got his Mum to walk behind him so that she was a little more sheltered from the battering wind. By the time they got to the first summit, at the radio transmitting station on Great Dun Fell, there was a total white out and Jane was on the verge of hyperthermia. Matthew got everyone into his storm tent and took the decision that the group would descend by the transmission centre's service road and would then get a lift round to that night's destination. At the time it was a bitter pill to swallow, but it was absolutely the right decision to make. Clearly the chap on the crutches at Complexo Xacbeo would have to come to his own decision about continuing or postponing his pilgrimage.

Day 35. June 5th Triacastela – Sarria   18.7K/11.7M (stayed at Carris Alphonso IX)

This was the day we would arrive in Sarria. This was the place that many people, particularly many Spanish, began the pilgrimage. If people walked just the last 100 kilometres to Santiago they could still claim a compostela or a certificate of completion. We came to understand that for some Spanish people it was considered a good thing to have done all or part of the Camino Way, that it looked good on a curriculum vitae when applying for jobs and for some young people it was a bit like the British "Duke of Edinburgh Award Scheme" that encourages a range of activities, including an expedition. This last section was also a very "do-able" length for charity fund raising. We were expecting the character of the pilgrimage to possibly change as new pilgrims arrived without the experiences under their belts that the longer-distance pilgrims had. To an extent that is exactly what happened; the character did change. This was a consequence of the very different terrain we were walking through as much as the noisy exuberance of large parties of Spanish pilgrims. We had found at all stages of the pilgrimage that the Spanish pilgrims en mass are very loud. Jane likened their conversations to round singing. One would start talking, then the companion would start talking over his/her friend, then the next in the party would start talking – all a little louder than the previous one in order to be heard – but no one appeared to be listening although everyone would be talking. This behaviour created such a racket that they could never hear another pilgrim approaching behind them and wanting to get past. It would mean we had to pick up pace hugely to swing out round them and overtake. These strange groups of shouting Spanish people increased in the Galician leg of the journey as, whilst there were not huge additional numbers, there were some.

The countryside we walked through was absolutely beautifully bucolic. There were rolling hills covered in pastures with cows grazing – a site we had not seen since the Pyrenees. We came across the prettiest little cows imaginable. Later we discovered they were called Cachena cattle and are one of the smallest breeds of cattle in the world and have long lyre-shaped horns. We came across a meadow of these cows, with a bull, many pregnant females and a cow that had clearly just given birth and was licking its wobbly little baby.

This day we also walked down a number of "hollow-ways" – tracks that had been worn down by the thousands of feet that had passed over them through the years such that the sides towered above the track. These hollow-ways were believed to be part of the original pilgrimage route. Many other parts of the ancient route have changed over the years to make way for developments, buildings, land purchase and environmental changes. It was quite moving to feel we were walking in the footsteps of the original pilgrims. We also started seeing strange tall and narrow storage sheds set up high on concrete or stone bases. We spent many a happy hour speculating on their purpose. Many were made with slatted wood, so surely rodents would get in and eat produce stored inside. As they were so tall, perhaps they were for tobacco leaves to hang and dry (we had seen many market gardens with large plots of a huge leafed plant that we could not identify, but thought might be tobacco). They were too odd a shape to be wine stores or oil stores. In a macabre moment we thought there might be a Galician custom of keeping the urns of ones dearly departed in these constructions. Many properties had one of these storage sheds, whether the property was a farm, small-holding or a private domestic dwelling. One could clearly buy ornamental versions at the garden centre as we saw some of those as well. This is what they looked like, although some could be very ornate.

Earlier we had walked with a Spanish man, Rafael from Madrid. He had worked in the television industry but had been made redundant and was passing some time by doing part of the Camino Way. Later he hoped to set up a book shop café with friends using his redundancy money. We bumped into Rafael a bit over the next couple of days. He enlightened us with respect to these funny sheds. They were called horreos, with an almost silent, slightly guttural "H", and were used as granaries. The slats on the sides allowed for ventilation whilst the overhanging pedestal support prevented rodents getting in – so much for the domestic mausoleum theory! Quite why they were so elaborately constructed and so tall and skinny just to store corn-on-the-cob was not obvious.

Rafael had brilliant English as he had worked both in America and England. We teased him about some of his English pronunciation, but then he looked blankly uncomprehending when we told him about what we had decided to do when we had arrived at Sahagun - when Charlotte had shin splints – he simply could not understand us. We cannot replicate here phonetically how we should have pronounced "Sahagun"; suffice to say we were way off the mark. Over the next couple of days we both became very worried about Rafael spending his redundancy money on a bookshop at a time when the world was moving to internet shopping for its books. This worry was exacerbated as he had told us the shop was to concentrate on the detective novel genre – this seemed very niche to us. On another day when we met up we were relieved to hear that they had thought through where to locate the bookshop and that they would have a café to draw people in. We sincerely hope Rafael finds success in whatever venture he embarks on.

There was a long hot plod finally into Sarria along a roadside with nowhere to rest. We hunkered down with Rafael on some tree stumps on a verge and were ecstatic to discover in Jane's pack two cartons of fruit juice we had entirely forgotten – they were much needed and appreciated. Once we arrived in the town, we spent some time taking the last photos for a blog we were going to write on how pilgrims find their way across northern Spain.

We were pleased to arrive at our destination – a nice hotel – and quickly did the whole bath and laundry routine. We decided to eat a lunch instead of dinner as both meals are served far later than their equivalents in England. Charlotte had to honour her pledge to eat pulpo in Sarria, and she did. She said it tasted not bad at all. We had to go to an internet café to do the blog and despite there being serried ranks to choose from, the computers were all ancient, over-used and very slow. We persevered and eventually got the navigation blog posted.

Blog (Jane) Wednesday, 5 June 2013 Every Which Way

Jane: I am sure some of you have been wondering how Charlotte and I have managed to find our way almost 500 miles across northern Spain without Henry to point the way with his sat map. Well it has been pretty difficult I can tell you. We have had to draw on all our collective map reading, trail finding and orienteering skills. Thank goodness we both got our tracking badges in the Girl Guides.

We recognise the value that Girl Guide training has had, but we need also to thank Ray Meers for all his survival tips and in particular we are so glad we spent hours as children watching the Lone Ranger. Tonto's tracking tips have proved invaluable -- many a time we have had our ear to the track listening for the distance tramp of pilgrims' feet.

Particularly useful have been such aids to direction as the sun, obviously, but when cloudy we frequently looked for the mossy side of the trees, put a wet finger to the wind, looked for the angle of bushes in the prevailing wind and occasionally came across the spoor of pilgrims who had gone ahead: the bent grass, the broken twig, the tell-tale toilet paper --- all helped keep us on the true path. Just now and again, alert for signs, we might glimpse a small yellow direction arrow such as this one:

We have needed to keep our wits about us as when deep in contemplation it is easy to miss the discreet and simple way marks as you can see below:

204

If we were very lucky we occasional found little primitive indicators on the ground that suggested we were on the right path:

Once in a while we might find a larger sign:

Of course we also kept our eyes peeled in case we spotted any other pilgrims who might indicate the way:

In a very few places the local authorities have invested in the odd sign or two:

As you can see it has been very difficult to keep to The Way and our early training in trail finding continues to prove invaluable. Every day we put into practice our fine-honed inner compasses:

You may have guessed ---- you have to be a complete idiot to get lost

We have to thank this gentleman, Don Elias Valina Sampedro, (above) for inventing the Camino Way yellow arrow system. These arrows are pretty much everywhere.

So, five days to go- blog when we can. Thanks for all your lovely comments -many a chuckle at this end. By the way, Charlotte´s new favourite dish is pulpo (look it up) but only when she can sucker it off the plate!

Day 36. June 6th Sarria – Portomarin 22.4K/14M (stayed at Ferramenteiro Albergue)

The temperature was cooler on this day as we set off after breakfast looking forward to another lovely pastoral walk. Much of the countryside we walked through was as delightful as the previous day's and we were so happy to see storks again, this time foraging in a field.

We walked up through woodland where we met a Spanish chap seemingly living rough but offering to stamp pilgrim credencials for a donation. He had a tent available for pilgrims to sleep in if they wanted – enterprising, but a bit close to Sarria. We began to see the "count down" concrete kilometre signs. There was a real sense that it was all coming to a conclusion although the city of Santiago still felt a long distance away; it felt very rural where we were walking.

There were a reasonable number of pilgrims on the path this day, but it was not as crowded as we thought it would be. We were stepping out happily in the mild temperature on a flat gravel path whose verges were filled with wild flowers, including banks of foxgloves. Jane was ahead, Charlotte behind. All of a sudden a noise made Jane turn around – immediate emergency action was required as Charlotte was flat on her face, crumpled into the verge. Jane shouted for her to stay still as she ran back and as pilgrims behind and in front all ran to give aid. Having climbed the Pyrenees, the Alto del Perdon, La Cruz de Ferro and O'Cebreiro, Charlotte had managed to slip on a completely flat bit of path. All should have been well after the initial shock except that her left wrist had been bent under by the loop on her walking pole. After the offers to ring for help had been turned down and we had reassured people all was well, Jane got Charlotte to her feet and it was clear that all was not in fact well; Charlotte's wrist and hand were useless and very painful. We had three and a half days to complete the pilgrimage so we knew in our hearts we could not risk a hospital visit as this would throw us entirely. Charlotte was game to continue. We collapsed one of Charlotte's poles and continued until we came to a bar. It was obvious Charlotte was very shocked and in a lot of pain so Jane bought coffee and cake, got out the anti-inflammatory pills and the crepe bandage Henry had insisted we took with us. We sat for a while joined by a lovely woman from London, but originally from Rwanda and by the owner's huge salivating dog – well we had the cake, but he wanted it.

A brief aside about dogs: we had read a bit before we left on this adventure that walking poles and pilgrims' staffs could be useful for fending off the many "wild dogs" one came across in Spain. We have to report that we did see quite a lot of dogs, usually around the semi-deserted villages, hardly ever in the truly open countryside. These dogs were often of a type of Alsatian breed or a sort of huge, broad hound (we are not dog people so we had to guess at what they were). They were almost always very big and loped around, often in small groups. Charlotte had said that as we were the "pack leaders" we should show our disdain for the humble pack members by not even deigning to give them eye contact. This would tell them they were insignificant and they would slope off. Initially it took a bit of courage to do this: peering off into the distance in the opposite direction to the dogs until we had walked past them, but it worked, or at least it appeared to work. We had a real sense that these dogs were not remotely interested in the passing pilgrims. They were probably all farm dogs or even domestic dogs – not wild at all. Many of them were comatose and did not bother to even lift a sleepy head to see who was passing by. We could understand how, if someone was frightened of dogs, that their size could be worrying. We did not hear a single tale en route of anyone being bothered by, leave alone attacked by these beasts.

Back to our new drama: we now had to continue our walk to Portomarin along undulating paths and then down into the valley to the little town. We passed through a tiny village where the cows were slowly meandering and stopping to investigate possible food stuffs in gardens and along hedges. The cowherds were in no hurry and were happy to let their herd take all the time in the world to move through the village. We just had to watch where we put our feet. This was a 14 mile day so we were going to be reasonably tired by the end of the walk – and we were. The tiredness seemed to be accumulating; we were not shrugging it off in the same way we had at the start of the journey.

We arrived at the broad river Mino and crossed it on a wide road bridge. This was such a long bridge with a walkway at the edge and so high above the river, it was easy to get vertigo slowly walking across.

On the far side of the bridge we discovered a towering flight of steps we then had to climb. In the 1960's the whole village of Portomarin and been relocated to higher ground to allow for the building of a reservoir. The Church of San Juan was one of the old buildings moved brick by brick to its new location. We had to climb up to this higher level. The albergue we were staying at was huge, very clean, very well appointed and with young hospitaleros "policing" all the time. The wash rooms were vast and single-sex and impeccably clean. The sleeping area was like a hangar with serried ranks of metal bunk beds with a curtain across after every third row. People were already sleeping – we found that a lot: people got in early and went to sleep. We tended to avoid doing that as we slept so badly at night as it was despite being exhausted.

Charlotte was now faced with the real challenge of operating single-handedly. Undressing, showering, dressing, unpacking is all considerably more difficult with only one hand, even with Jane doing all the buttons up for her. The re-usable "ice bandage" we had bought at Trabadelo for Charlotte's shin splints now came in very handy for reducing the swelling on her wrist. Before going out to explore we decided that we needed to splint Charlotte's wrist; it was very swollen and extremely painful and Charlotte (rightly as it turned out) felt it needed to be immobilised. We put our thinking caps on in terms of the kit we had and how to improvise a splint. Charlotte then had a Eureka moment remembering the sporks she had bought each of us. A spork is a double ended eating implement, with a spoon at one end and a fork at the other facing the opposite way. Sporks are useful bits of camping equipment, but they also make very good wrist splints. With the fork end, tines facing out, in the palm of her hand and the spoon end on her wrist and the crepe bandage wrapping it all tightly, Charlotte could not move the wrist at all. On our return to England we went to a hospital and got the wrist x-rayed and sure enough, as in our heart of hearts we suspected, Charlotte had broken her wrist. The fracture consultant was very complimentary of our Heath Robinson first aid as he said that normally with the type of break she had he would have operated and put a pin in, but as it was there was no need as the break was beginning to mend well and correctly. There appear to be several morals here: for goodness sake do not let foxgloves distract you from the important things in life like maintaining your balance; random bits of kitchen ware can be "life-savers".

We went into the village to explore and find somewhere for an early supper. The church, which had been moved brick by brick to its current location, was a somewhat unprepossessing building from the outside. We were amazed that it was open and we could go inside. There we discovered an incredibly elongated figure of the Virgin Mary. This in itself was a little aesthetically odd, but what was more unusual was that the statue was dressed in real clothes: a long silky white dress with a pale blue cloak and a long lace veil. It all looked pristine so we guessed that the clothes must be changed fairly regularly to keep them dust free. It was unusual. In the cathedral in Astorga we had seen a Christ Child with real hair draped over his head which we had found very creepy. This statue here, in contrast looked quite elegant, if a little tall. We bumped into Peter and Alma from Wales whom we had met at breakfast that morning in Sarria. They had just started their week long pilgrimage. We ate an early supper together outside at a slightly quaint Italian café – lovely to eat proper pasta (a staple for Jane back home as her mother-in-law was Italian). We then updated the blog on a slow old computer at the hostel

Our allocated bunk was free-standing, in other words not against the wall. It had short bars on the top bunk at the head end which proved to be a challenge to Jane that night as her legs kept slipping off the bed altogether, occasionally almost followed by the rest of her. Next to us was a lady called Carole who was from New Hampshire. She was lovely and we chatted that evening and at breakfast and walked together for a while the following day. Carole told us of the only cases of theft amongst pilgrims that we heard of: her sunglasses being taken by another pilgrim as she went to a bar and her seeing them in his top pocket and a Korean girl's money being taken from her bunk.

Blog (Jane) Thursday, 6 June 2013: Not a holiday but a journey

First an update: my theory is that Charlotte could not wait to kiss the holy soil of Santiago de Compostela, or maybe she just wanted to get some practice in -- anyway, I'm walking along and behind me Charlotte is lying flat on her face on the path! She said she was just admiring some fox gloves!?! The result of this "little slip" is one sprained left wrist which is now splinted with one of our sporks and the crepe bandage Henry insisted Jane pack. Charlotte is fine to finish, but Jane has to do up her buttons!

There have been a few comments from our nearest and dearest about holiday snaps (and how you cannot wait to see the full set). We need to point out that this six week period has not been a holiday (we'll have one of those when we return), but it has been a journey.

It has been a journey through four distinct provinces in Spain with varied scenery, weather, wines, wild flowers, farming to name but a few of the differences. It has also been a journey of discovery for us: learning about Spain, about ourselves, about coping in adversity, about friendships.

There have been many occasions when we have not taken pictures so we cannot share all our experiences with you. Sometimes it was simply too wet to get the camera out, too muddy to risk any unnecessary movement, too steep to risk taking our hands off our poles, or too fleeting for us to capture that moment. However, here are a few pictures we would like to share:

A deeply green river and a rather lovely bridge (Puenta La Reina).

Communal meals with other pilgrims - always lovely experiences. This is the place where we had to "sing for our supper"

An example of the strange pilgrim practice of putting crosses on wire fences, particularly next to main roads -- always looked very macabre.

Some pilgrims clearly have too much energy. All along The Way there are little art constructions -- usually small towers of round stones, or way markers decorated with stones and flowers, or large arrows made from pine cones, orange peel, or whatever comes to hand. This was a rather more aesthetically pleasing example. Charlotte and I were always too kn.....d to do much more than take a photo.

Cyclists are catered for as you can see from this bridge with its useful bike ramp.

Many people do the Camino Way on bikes. A few will ring their bell or bellow "Buen Camino" as they fly past frightening the wits out of us. We are amazed that there appear to be no collisions between walkers and riders.

We have largely eaten "the pilgrim meal" each day. A three course set menu at a modest price. We did, however, push the boat out in Burgos where Charlotte ordered the roast lamb. As you can see, not a scrap of mint sauce, nor a vegetable in sight -- just a leg of lamb and a little lamb's tail.

We loved the beautiful, gentle cows in the Pyrenees. After that we barely saw any livestock anywhere. It was a joy to move into Galicia where we have seen so many fat, well-cared for cattle including these ones with the most amazing horns. There was one mother licking her hour-old wobbly-kneed babe.

Galicia is famous for its pulpo. Here Charlotte honours her pledge that she would eat pulpo in Sarria. We were ages waiting while the chef prepared the dish; it took hours to cook as it kept turning the gas off (boom, boom)!

Ever mindful of the needs of weary pilgrims who had walked 14 miles, the good people of Portomarin make you climb these!

Glorious cold weather! (Earlier on) Perhaps we should explain the expressions in our photos. However exhausted we felt, we always said when taking photos, "Don´t look so tired!"

One of the few dry days on the Meseta after a period of continuous rain.

Very recently here in Galicia we have been walking on the original and very ancient Camino Way. Often we are walking along hollow ways worn down by the feet of countless pilgrims over the centuries. Sometimes the original walls are way above one's head. They are cool and atmospheric.

Jane arriving at Portomarin today and barely remembering the rule about not looking tired!

Day 37. June 7th Portomarin – Palas de Rei   24.8K/15.5M (stayed at Albergue Buen Camino)

It was a difficult day today. We were both a bit out of sorts after a poor night's sleep and the aches and pains for both of us had accumulated now and of course, Charlotte had to contend with her aching wrist and Jane with the extra little chores. It was raining as we set out at 07.40, which is always a bit of a morale downer. The walking however, was pleasant for the most part. We stopped at a lovely albergue just to rest and fill our water bottles. It was run by American volunteers and exuded a really happy atmosphere. We discovered that the day before, when Charlotte had her fall, two other women had also had accidents: one we saw walking covered in grazes; another was waiting for a taxi as she could not continue on her sprained ankle. That gravel had clearly had some ultra-slippery quality to it! A large German lady who had been very solicitous of Charlotte the day before came and enquired as to how she was faring. We would see this lady all the way to Santiago and she made a great friendly fuss every time we bumped into her. She herself had set out the previous year to walk the Camino Way but had had an accident almost as soon as she began so this was her second attempt and she was very close to achieving her goal. We said farewell to Carole from New Hampshire – she was one of the very fleeting, but lovely friendships on the Way.

When we finally reached Palas de Rei after a 15.5 mile walk, we were disappointed with the town – no king's palace here, but many dull buildings and too many cars. The albergue was moderately grim as well despite it being a private hostel. Charlotte was clearly incapacitated to an extent, but the hostel manager made no offer to help Jane get the two big rucksacks up three flights of stairs. We were shown our bunks and our hearts dropped to discover we had been allocated a bunk in a room full of children. There were eight very young Spanish teenagers in the room, five boys, three girls. They were doing the final part of the Camino Way as part of a school project. They were very polite but kids have to be kids, chatting, playing their music and playing "musical bunk beds". There was clearly one couple, a girl and a boy, who spent a lot of time in a top bunk together whilst the others piled like puppies on each other's bunks. They were in awe of how far we had walked as they were going in very short stages (to extend the fun?) of around eight miles a day. We felt like their grannies and were very aware that they probably did not want their grannies in their bedroom at any time, leave alone on this adventure. We got ourselves sorted out as usual but after Jane discovered the communal showers were miniscule with nowhere to hang anything, she advised Charlotte to skip the shower. The tiny washroom area was dirty and poorly equipped. We found a bar where everyone was watching Rafa Nadal win a tennis match on TV and where we were able to do a brief blog update. We went out to eat that evening not wanting to spend a single additional euro in this unpleasant albergue. We were aware of the irony of having nearly finished the pilgrimage but continuing to be very critical.

Blog (Jane) Friday, 7 June 2013   *Mini-blog - Hi folks! Very tiring walk today but weather held off. Long day tomorrow and we shall have to creep out of our dormitory (which is full of 15 year old Spanish children) very early to cope with the distance. We are both very tired now and because we know the end is near, it seems to make each day a little harder.*

To be positive, however, Charlotte's spork splint is working and whilst her wrist is very swollen and painful, it is not getting any worse.

We hope to do a proper blog in a couple of days as we need to share with you a very strange and continuous occurrence that we have not yet told you about. This is very brief as circumstances don't allow for a longer blog. Love to all. J and C

Day 38. June 8th Palas de Rei – Ribadiso – 25.8K/16.1M (stayed at Los Caminantes Albergue)

This was a long day and we had our ponchos on most of the time, either fully or as cloaks; the sky remained dark and threatening almost the entire way. We crept out in the dark not waking any of the children – not as easy as previous 06.00 starts as Jane had to help Charlotte and do two trips down and up the three flights of stairs to get the packs down, but we managed. We were glad to leave Palas de Rei, but we did want some breakfast. We stopped at the first open place, a bar on a main road. There we met an interesting character; an American who had been involved in a terrible accident back home. He had been riding his horse when it was spooked by a lorry cutting in far too close. By the time the horse had stopped bolting, the American had sustained multiple life-threatening injuries and it was uncertain he would survive. Clearly, he had survived but with all sorts of bits of metal in him, including in his legs. He could walk short distances without crutches but needed them for any sort of lengthy walking. He had started his pilgrimage at St Jean Pied de Port, the same as us – it was staggering to think how he had managed it. We saw him a fair bit that day; he loped along swinging between the two crutches moving far faster than either of us. He intended to continue down into Portugal after getting to Santiago and had arranged with other pilgrims he had met along the way to meet up the following year to walk the Great Wall of China after having raised individual contributions to charity. We got the impression that he just wanted to keep on walking and never stop.

This day's walk required us to cross five little rivers along the way. It was a bit like coastal walking: reasonably flat for the most part, but then short steep descents followed by short steep ascents to accommodate the bays (or in our case, the rivers). In the dark we walked through a little village and saw our very first statue of a female pilgrim; she was dancing with her partner. We were pleased to see her given the number of women on the Way. We also saw yet more

224

pilgrim art work; a perfect circle of multi-coloured flower petals positioned across the entire path with little gaps for walkers to pass through. This piece of art was in a wood where there were only trees so the petals would have had to brought in by the pilgrim. They were all colours: orange, pink, white, purple. Usually the pilgrim artwork is made up of the materials lying around: stones, sticks, lavender and other wild flowers. This flower circle was different as it seemed very pre-meditated but was in such a random place – we almost trod all over it as it was so dark and gloomy. Well, as they say in Yorkshire, "None so queer as folk"!

We were very, very tired this day. It was almost as if the closer we got to Santiago, the further away it felt and the wearier we became. Psychologically we would have expected to be re-energised as we were now so close. We stopped at a village bar to get some artificial energy. At the counter Jane was amazed to see a giant version of the pan di spagna cake Henry's mother, Maria, made at home. In recipe books this cake is described as an Italian sponge cake, which it is. However, it is very different to the usual British sponge as it is very light and airy from the enormous number of eggs in it and has a crusty top from the sugar. Maria would describe how this cake was made for special occasions and several women would bake together taking it in turns to beat the eggs and sugar (as, of course, there were no electrical whisks back then). Maria used to make one for Jane's son, Matthew, to take back to university with him and he would eat the whole thing before he arrived there. Jane asked permission to take a photo as the cake was so enormous. The lady who had baked it, clearly flattered by the attention then took a photo of us.

The oh-so-necessary coffee and pan di spagna cake break.

We passed through the town of Melide which we thought was another ugly town. The villages in between were all very pretty. Perhaps we had just become too sensitised to towns and only felt comfortable walking in the country side or in villages. We still had two more rivers to cross so we plodded on. The weather was even more threatening by the time we eventually arrived at Ribadiso, our day's destination. This village was a tiny, neat little place just on the far side of the final little river. The albergue was a private hostel and our room had just four bunks in it. The bathroom had two tiny showers, one toilet and a basin. Despite there being two showers one could only use the facilities with a friend or by one's self as the showers were too tiny to undress or dress in. This was no problem for us, but it was for Colm, the Irish chap in our room. He had been crossing his legs for ages whilst two French women were showering so we suggested he knocked and shouted that he was coming in with his eyes closed. It seemed to work – no international incident ensued.

This Irish pilgrim, Colm, had started from Sarria and had intended to walk with his partner. Just before their departure date her foot was run over (twice!!) by a car in their village as they were attending a music festival, but she insisted Colm went despite her not being able to. He told us that his forebears had come from Galicia many hundreds of years before and that there was a strong Celtic link between Ireland and Galicia – hence all the "O's" in front of the place names in Galicia. We left Colm to doze in the little tent he had made in his bunk by draping his poncho along the side. We donned our ponchos as it was pouring with rain and we went to check out the bar over the road. Charlotte found a table and Jane went to get drinks.

Whilst Jane was waiting to be served a man came up behind her smiling broadly and greeting her; it took her a while to realise it was Michael from California whom we had met with Ayn so frequently in the early part of the pilgrimage, but had not seen since Torres del Rio on May 10th, our day eight. We had been convinced that they were both way ahead of us or alternatively, that they had returned home because of Ayn's health. It was absolutely lovely to see them again. We sat together to catch up and shared a few of our adventures. The picture of Ayn and Michael below (permission given for its use) may show them looking a little strained. This is because they were telling us about a really frightening adventure they had between Boadillo and Fromista when they had become inadvertently separated and lost each other. Eventually all was resolved, but we were sad to hear that pilgrims had not come to Ayn's aid, but instead she had to rely on the aid of the local police who were extremely helpful. We were also sad to hear this tale as Boadillo had been an entrancing place for us; beautiful and gentle and friendly with the never-to-be-forgotten swallow and martin formation flying displays. We could not have been far apart from Ayn and Michael and we hated to think that we were relaxing and enjoying ourselves whilst they were desperately trying to find each other and Ayn was imagining the worst had happened to her husband. Over the final two days we met up along the walk and shared a hostel together.

Reunion with Ayn and Michael at Ribadiso

Day 39. June 9th Ribadiso – O Pedrouzo (Arca) 22.1 K/13.8M (stayed at O Burgo)

We were off early the next day wearing ponchos under a heavy sky for our penultimate day's walk. The mist hung low over Ribadiso as we climbed up from the little village by the river. This day was the day of the eucalyptus woods, an everyday sight for many of the

Australians on the Way, but a complete novelty to us. We walked through both small and large eucalyptus woods, some where the trees were so immensely tall with the branches meeting over our heads and the strong eucalyptus aroma perfuming the air – it felt like walking through a living cathedral. The ground was strewn with the fallen blossoms – little fluffy white flowers You can get an impression of their size if you try to find the little figure in the picture below.

Great strips of the peeled bark lay all over the path as did the white fluffy blossoms. As we tramped over this debris even more of the perfume was released into the air. We knew that these trees were a contributor to the huge fires that sometimes swept across parts of Australia, but we thought they were awesome.

Despite our tiredness and the increasing aches and pains, we made good progress, walking the first 10 kilometres without really realising it. We had one stop for coffee, unlike the day before when we needed to stop any number of times. It was the second 10 K that we found difficult as we kept mis-reading the guide book and so thought we were further along than in fact we were. Having left that morning at 07.25, we arrived at the albergue, O'Borgo at 14.40. We had our own room and bathroom – lovely. The place was very neat and clean, but also very cold. We laundered the minimum number of items necessary and draped them round the room then went to the bar next door to find something to eat.

The lady in the bar was charming and despite its being too late for lunch and too early for dinner, she was happy to serve us a pilgrim's menu meal. It was lovely and warm so we stayed there a while finalising our plan for our penultimate blog.

We intend no offence to anyone; the blog was meant as a small homage.

Blog (Jane and Charlotte) Sunday, 9 June 2013 The Virtual Pilgrim

Hi everyone! This will be our penultimate blog as we get into Santiago de Compostela tomorrow (hopefully). We are rather staggered that we have actually got this far - and some of you might share that feeling about us - but here we are. The reality is that we have felt hugely buoyed up by the support we have received throughout our huge adventure from all our friends and relations that we know have been following the blog, making comments, sending us texts or emails or simply wishing us well over the ether.

In addition to all that (oh so appreciated) support, we have also felt very supported by The Way itself. There is a sort of pilgrim presence that follows you along The Way and spurs you on when you flag and helps you solve the inevitable problems that occur. It is difficult to put this "presence" into words; to try to describe such an ephemeral support is not easy. When we have felt low (not often, but it has happened now and again) the "presence" of The Way has at times surrounded us with support or sent "messages" that gave us courage.

The pilgrim "presence" has given sustenance, shelter and spiritual comfort, in particular at times when we have struggled physically, emotionally and mentally and in particular when we have doubted our abilities and strengths to complete The Way. The Pilgrim "presence" has smoothed our path, ethereally offered words of advice and solace. We can only give you a flavour of this very real support and comfort in the following few photos:

The "presence" at first was shadowy and discreet:

Gradually the "presence" would peer from afar, guiding our feet

We both felt surrounded by the "presence":

The "presence" often felt like a wise advisor

At other times the "presence" was there in the background -- to be lent on if needed

The amorphous support offered by the "presence" gave us heart when days were long.

We often felt the pilgrim "presence" was virtually sharing a drink or two with us:

Every day the pilgrim "presence" popped up and reminded us of where we were going and where we would return to

Quite often the pilgrim "presence" reminded us to rest and provided us with the will and way to find succour.

The pilgrim "presence" was always a robust support and we drew strength from his strength.

Throughout the journey the support continued to surround us:

The very real nearness gave heart when heart was needed.

The pilgrim "presence" encouraged us to stride forth and believe we could achieve our goal.

The "presence" was ever there to be lent on and offer a guiding hand.

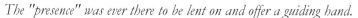

The *"presence"* looked ahead and seemed to offer advice to ease our onward journey:

When confused or puzzled the *"presence"* offered clarity and direction:

Both Charlotte and I have great gratitude and love for this constant pilgrim presence that has enabled us to almost complete this adventure of a life time, walking the Camino Way.

Of course some of you will already have realised who the Virtual Pilgrim is

Not San Jacobo but: ....

Our darling Henry!

Thank you, thank you, thank you a million times for enabling me/ us to do this trip, holding the fort whilst also giving so much support both practical and emotional. Tomorrow -- Santiago!

CHAPTER TEN   EXHAUSTION AND EUPHORIA

Day 40. June 10th O Pedrouzo – Santiago de Compostela 20.1K/12.6M (stayed at Hostal dos Reyes Catolicos)

The final day of walking and ponchos were on our backs again. We had to put on wet tops as the laundry had not dried in the cold room. Jane wanted to complete the walk as she had begun it - with a full rucksack. She re-claimed her sleeping bag, spare clothes and wash stuff from Charlotte's sack and stood amazed at how she had ever carried this beast up the Pyrenees and all the way to Leon. On one level the walk was enjoyable. There was a sort of feeling that we must savour all aspects as this was the end. On another level, we were so tired that we were desperate to complete the walk as quickly as possible. The first stage of the day was like many previous days: eucalyptus trees and countryside. Even when we slowly walked past Santiago's airport, we could hear but not see the planes and we still felt it was very rural. It did not become busy and urbanised until the final five kilometres. We stopped at a bar in a little village for some refreshments and bumped into Meg, the young American studying in London whom we had met in Ponferrada and who was flying back on the same fight as us. We exchanged numbers and arranged to share a taxi to the airport in two days' time. We also saw here the young English girl who had been receiving much attention from the piratical French guy from Marseilles way back at Villafranca Montes de Oca on our day 14. She was tucking into bacon and eggs and had clearly managed her solo pilgrimage successfully.

Before we left the village, we called in at the little church and got our credencial stamped. The advice to pilgrims starting their pilgrimage from Sarria was to get their credencial stamped at least twice each day. This was to provide evidence that the pilgrim had walked the

Way rather than taken a bus. We were unsure whether this rule applied to people who had set off further away, but we did not risk it so made sure we had our two stamps each day. As we left we saw ahead of us a strange little group we had first seen back in Sarria and then again in Palas de Rei. The group consisted of a Mum, a Dad and a baby; sometimes the baby was carried and at other times it was in the pram. On this occasion the hill was so steep to climb up out of the village, Dad was pushing the pram up the hill with a huge pack on his back and another in the buggy, whilst Mum carried the baby. We had to take our hats off to them as it was a tough enough journey for an individual without having to see to the needs of a baby as well.

We had one plodding climb to complete before the "downhill all the way" bit. This was Monte del Gozo. It was a gentle climb really and once at the top we could see Santiago de Compostela below us. The mount was a slightly bizarre place with very little "soul". There was a snack shack and a monstrous great block of "art" on the scrubby top. Beauty is in the eye of the beholder and art is a very subjective thing, but this monument to the Camino Way was, in our view, not very aesthetically pleasing.

We set off down. The last five kilometres seemed to go on for ever through the suburbs of Santiago. We just put our heads down and plodded. Eventually we came into the old part of the town. The pilgrim does not get any sense of approaching the cathedral – the final destination of all the pilgrims. We sort of fell across the cathedral, coming to it from the side. Having climbed down the steps at the side of the cathedral we could see its famous frontage and really feel that we had arrived. It was mizzling with rain but we did not care. There were few pilgrims around and certainly no one we knew so we had our own private little "whoopee"! It was a very strange moment. In the blog below posted the following day you can see photos of us, tired but very happy. We did a whole bunch of stuff after this, getting our compostela, checking into the hotel, bathing and having one celebratory drink – this was too much. At 19.30, after one small glass of Cava, we fell sound asleep. We missed the texts from Henry saying Michael and Ayn had emailed with details about a celebratory meal that night. We woke at 23.30pm unable to believe we had completed our 500 mile journey.

Blog Tuesday, 11 June 2013   End of the Road

Jane and Charlotte:

Well we got here! We were totally exhausted upon our arrival yesterday afternoon. The last day of walking was not really any different from all the many, many preceding days, but in fact it felt different -- longer and more wearisome. It was almost as if our bodies knew it was the last day of walking, but instead of being enervated they just objected.

We arrived in front of the cathedral in the mizzling rain, queued at the Pilgrims' office to get our compostela and checked into the Parador Hotel -- bliss! Bath - bliss! Sleep -- bliss! One glass of cava -- zonk!

Today was a better, but more emotional day as we went to the pilgrims´ mass and met some of the people we had met along The Way. We were both surprised at how emotionally teary we felt. We were not the only ones like this - quite a few people were quietly weeping at different times. Everybody had been on their own journey for their own reasons and now it has perhaps ended, perhaps continues, perhaps begins again.

Some folks we have met along The Way are continuing to the coast - to Finisterre (once believed to be the actual end of the world). We have no desire whatsoever to continue walking. In fact a mooch round the shops was just delightful.

In one of our early blogs we gave you five words from each of us that described how we felt about The Camino Way at that time. We have now individually determined on five words each that describe what the Way has meant to us at its end. Here they are:

Charlotte: *painful, indescribable, unique, arduous and over.*	**Jane:** *exhausting, adventurous, transient, emotional and confirmatory.*

Are we different, better, nicer people after having completed this 500 mile (did you get that? 500 mile!!!!!) pilgrimage? Well, you'll have to let us know. We look the same.

This way to Santiago!

"I am sure this is still the way."

4.7 kilometres from the cathedral -- might as well have been 10.7!!

Monte del Gozo

What a facade!! -- I mean the cathedral.

Euphoria!

Well -- would we advise any of you to do this trip? We are not sure -- it has been very strange. NOT like walking in the Lakes or the Dales -- a little like the West Highland Way but with more towns and more deserted villages and six times longer.

We have learnt an awful lot: about packing, Camino fashion, wild flowers, making and leaving friends, climbing out of top bunks, Spanish landscape, Spanish weather, impromptu laundry, the lingo, how much we miss and love our family and friends.

This is our last blog from Spain and we want to really, really sincerely thank you for bothering to read it and to leave comments, texts and emails. Thank you.

There has been a delightful, easy little greeting that all pilgrims use that can mean "hello", "goodbye", "go carefully", "enjoy yourself" -- almost anything you like. We must have heard it and said it 1,000 times so we say as our farewell to you all:

"Buen Camino!"

As the blog says, the day after our arrival was, in some ways, a more emotional day than the arrival day. We attended the pilgrims' mass along with many pilgrims who had recently completed the pilgrimage. It was difficult to find a seat at first, but we eventually did. We were all told, in various languages, not to take photos during the mass and of course no one did. A nun with a beautiful voice rehearsed the congregation in all the sung responses and throughout the service she sung beautifully. Towards the end of the service, the Korean man next to Jane, who had had great difficult standing at all and was swaying with tiredness, broke down completely and just sat and sobbed. Jane put a hand on his shoulder to comfort him, although he was probably just overwhelmed rather than sad. We were then treated to a bit of pure theatre – the swinging of the botafumeiro, the enormous incense burner, or thurible that had traditionally been swung to fumigate the cathedral because of the stench of the pilgrims. As one the congregation got out their cameras and started taking photos and videos; it was almost impossible not to. Eight men in monk-like brown robes swung the incense holder high into the vaults of the cathedral. The botafumeiro itself was half the size of a man and the flames were visible as it soared above our heads. Incense filled the cathedral. Apparently it is one of the largest incense censers in the world. We had not expected to see this event as we had heard that it was only done on special days or when there had been a donation to cover the cost. We had no idea whether anyone had made such a donation, but if they had, we were very grateful.

We had Charlotte's final holy medal to secrete in the Cathedral as per her original plan. But where to put it? We walked around the Cathedral a number of times seeking a suitable resting place where the medal would not be disturbed, but where it could rest for years with all Charlotte's anxieties about her childhood religion attached to it. Eventually, Charlotte chose an enormous stone sarcophagus with ancient runic script on its side. This stone monument would never be moved for dusting. The medal fitted neatly in the space between the tomb and the wall – it could rest undisturbed. Charlotte felt tired, emotional but at peace.

We met up with Ayn and Michael at the cathedral and heard about the celebratory meal we had missed. We later said our goodbyes to them. They were staying in Europe for some time and we were going home. We were sad to say farewell, but glad we had met up again. The two of us then "took off our pilgrim hats" and wandered round the many souvenir shops to find little things to bring back for the grandchildren. Jane also wanted to find a pilgrim statue as a thank you for Henry. This was not a difficult task. We had great fun before returning to the hotel for something to eat, to do our flight check in and organise a taxi.

The following day French air traffic control went on strike which meant no planes could fly over French airspace. The three of us (Meg joined us for the taxi trip to Santiago airport) had a three hour delay at the airport, but at least we had a flight. Henry collected us from the airport and then we were home. We spent a lot of time on our return doing practical things: Charlotte had child care duties and then had to sort out her fractured wrist; there were photos to sort out. Jane made a Camino slide show with appropriate walking-related accompanying soundtrack and also printed a photo book of some highlight photos. We told many people about the walk and Charlotte had a Camino dinner for friends. This was all a little like the stuff one does after any holiday. Life returned to its normal pattern with nothing very obvious having changed. However, the months went by and we both kept talking about the Camino Way, reminiscing and dwelling on it. We both felt it might be a good idea to try and pin down what the Camino Way had meant for us, both the prosaically physical and the more sublimely metaphysical – if we could. Hence we decided to write this book. The final chapter will try to summarise some of ways the Camino Way impacted on us.

CHAPTER ELEVEN   WHAT'S IT ALL ABOUT?

At the end of our first week we wrote five words each in our blog that summed up that week and then at the end of the adventure we each wrote another five words that characterised what the whole journey had meant to us.

First seven days in five words:

Charlotte's:	Jane's:
Surprising, Challenging, Scented, Extraordinary, Do-able	Discombobulating, Sensual, Challenging, Sociable, Foreign

We hope that it has become clear to the reader why we chose these first set of words as you have read through the book.

Final words to sum up the Camino Way:

Charlotte: painful, indescribable, unique, arduous and over.	Jane: exhausting, adventurous, transient, emotional and confirmatory.

Time has passed and now we can add to that list of words as, with more reflection, the Camino Way has come to mean more to us.

We think that as this is a book, full of words, key words such as those above, might be a way to get a handle on what the Camino Way meant to us at the time and what it continues to mean to us almost a year later. Some of the legacy of the 500 mile journey across northern Spain was of a very practical nature; other things we discovered or learnt were, and continue to be, of a more philosophical or psychological character. We went on a very particular journey, but we are sure some of the legacy for us will resonate with some readers who have experienced different types of "pilgrimages" in their own lives. One does not have to walk 500 miles to learn what we learnt, but for us the journey confirmed many things we knew already and clarified other things. We try to explain some of this through the semantic conceit of focusing on words that became important to us but which were suggested to us by the concept of who we were: "The Camino Way Pilgrims".

The Camino Way Pilgrims

Today, Tomorrow, Transience:

Today - Whilst actually walking each day on the 500 mile journey, we were very preoccupied with that day's requirements – almost entirely the requirements dictated by physical need. There was something very attractive about this "living for the moment" mentality. For much of the time we had no thought other than what we were doing at that moment; we could enjoy the immediacy entirely – not walking past something too busy to take notice. The burden of worrying about the future was lifted from our shoulders for the majority of the time that we were walking. Clearly we could only "live for today" because we had planned ahead to do this; we had saved up so we could afford the adventure; we had planned so that our responsibilities were covered while we were away; we had been the industrious and thoughtful "ants" so that on the walk we could spend some time being the thoughtless and joyful "grasshoppers". Obviously we cannot live our entire lives only living for "today", but there was something important about taking time every day to appreciate what we have, what and who is around us and to make the most of that day. Everyone has to think to the future, but what the Camino Way drove home to us was the need to try to be happy now and not to endlessly think that greater happiness and fulfilment will only come sometime in the future.

Tomorrow – Even whilst enjoying the intimacy of our surroundings because we had the luxury of experiencing everything around us as we slowly walked along, we did have to exercise some thought for the future – in particular, where we would sleep that night. At times Jane let that worry about the "tomorrow" take over and assume such huge proportions it squeezed out the enjoyment of the present. Her worry was then imparted to Charlotte who worried about keeping up the "charge to the next bed", but at the time was grateful that Jane was considering the "tomorrow". It might sound obvious to say one should try to balance the necessity of considering the future with the need to not let that future crowd out the current pleasures of the present. The Camino Way taught us that we must find some emotional equilibrium between the "living for today" and the "worrying about tomorrow" – not an easy thing to do in our normal lives – definitely a "working towards achieving it" lesson.

Transience – We have reported many times throughout this book the fleeting, but often significant meetings we enjoyed throughout the journey. Frequently these passing connections brought pleasure, amusement and companionship. Sometimes they provided information, reassurance and guidance. Often they came with fun and friendship. But then they were gone. This real but ephemeral camaraderie contained within it endless goodbyes and with those farewells came small sadnesses. Clearly it is possible to make new friends and keep those friends for a long time, but essentially the Camino Way "society" is made up of numerous short and momentary relationships. In many ways this was one of the important lessons of the Way: life is transient, passing – catch hold of one's joys and make the most of them.

All three of these words – today, tomorrow, transience – hold very powerful messages for both of us. We come from a family of worriers, but now in retirement must try to apply some of that Camino lesson - to appreciate a little more that the "now" is to be relished without letting concerns for the future spoil that enjoyment as it will all be gone in the blink of an eye.

The Camino Way Pilgrims

Hurts, Home:

Hurts - Compared to many travellers on the Camino Way that we had read about, heard of or whom we met, we suffered no physical hurts that prevented us completing our journey. Many pilgrims did go home. Charlotte's shin splints and broken wrist might have meant the curtailment or postponement of the adventure. Jane's chronic daily headache syndrome might have made it impossible to complete the pilgrimage. However, we coped with all these hurts – we found ways through these difficulties. We met many pilgrims on our route, nursing injuries sustained as they were walking; others had embarked with injuries they already had. They were, for the most part, ploughing on. There was a real lesson to us both that "where there is a will, there is a way". Because we so desperately wanted to complete the whole journey, we found ways to overcome or manage our hurts. However, there is a corollary to this lesson which is, that coping with the conundrum of continuing life with a hurt is made easier with the help of others - and sometimes that help is essential. Of course there are hurts that are not physical. We both hurt each other through tetchiness and lack of consideration. We felt assailed by the belligerent drunk man in Logroño. Charlotte felt hurt when seemingly friends had gone silent. Such emotional hurts need consideration and kindness to prevent in the first place and to mend them if they occur. Obviously this is not a new lesson for either of us, but there was something about the being "away from home and on our own – ness" of the Camino Way that made us more sensitive to the hurts we dish out to others to and that we receive without really intending to hurt.

Home – Although Jane had initiated the idea of doing the Camino Way pilgrimage, Charlotte had been equally as excited as Jane to embark on the adventure. Neither of us thought that we would miss our homes as much as we did – not just the physical comforts of our houses, but the families that made "home". Often when we returned from holidays in the past we would say it was lovely to be home, but whilst we had been away we had been immersed in the holiday and not really thinking of home. The Camino Way had been different: whilst we were on the Way we thought of home frequently and missed it terribly. Yes, we missed comfortable and clean bathrooms, but far more importantly we missed our loved ones. Trite though it may sound, home is where the heart is and those dear to us become much dearer in their absence. Even after almost a year when we could be forgiven for drifting back to being fed up with the usual irritations that all loved ones generate, we find it easy to remind ourselves of how much we missed them and thus forgive them more readily. We are a little more tolerant.

The Camino Way Pilgrims

Emotion:

Emotion – The Camino Way made us raw. We were exposed in a way that we normally did not experience in our home and professional lives. We were quicker to cry, quicker to make friends, quicker to laugh – more in touch with our feelings. In "normal" life we have to erect barriers as the world can be a hard and cruel place. Perhaps the lesson is about knowing when to let those barriers down and allow the emotion the upper hand – when to expose some of that "rawness".

The Camino Way Pilgrims

Cost, Caring, Challenge, Catholicism, Cathartic, Clarifying, Confirmatory:

Cost – There is clearly a financial cost to doing the Camino Way. This cost can be mitigated by only staying in municipal albergues or church albergues where a donation is given by the pilgrim. To cut costs one can buy one's own provisions and use the little kitchens that are available at some of the albergues and, clearly, one can minimise outlay at bars. However, one can compromise on all those economies of pilgrim life and make the journey a bit more comfortable (café con leche became an essential for us) but a bit more expensive. The degree of "financial compromise" one can and is prepared to make is a personal consideration. We had read about how one was not a "proper" pilgrim if one did not stay in the communal albergues; that one was not a "proper" pilgrim if one took a bus for a stage of the journey. Sometimes an additional cost to the "basic" pilgrimage was foist on us by the necessity of dealing with the hurts (injuries and illnesses) we had. Sometimes we compromised on a minimalist approach because we could – we had saved up for this journey. We were aware, however, of our lucky situation and it did make us want to be generous to others – in particular we were generous with offers of our first aid paraphernalia when we came across limping or distressed pilgrims. There were other costs – to those friends and family at home who had to pick up some of our responsibilities while we were away. When Jane got home she found her husband thinner and more tired than when she left. He had been very lonely despite being frenetically busy looking after his mum, the grandchildren and laying a network of drainage pipes in the garden. What was a real benefit to us – going on the pilgrimage – was not without its impact on other people. Again – the whole metaphor about ripples on the pond spreading out from one place and hitting a far shore elsewhere, or the butterfly flapping its wings creating some catastrophe far away, was not unknown to us – but perhaps we became more appreciative of that cost to others.

Caring – We have mentioned already how we had to take care of each other when accidents or illness occurred. We have written in a general way of how other pilgrims, for the most part, were caring of each other. There was a greater spontaneity in offering care to one another on the Way – we were all pilgrims together so people were less reserved than they might be in a broader population. A lesson we are trying to apply now the pilgrimage has ended is to spread that caring a little beyond our nearest and dearest who are usually the principal recipients. We are more aware of signs of distress shown by strangers and are more open to offering assistance.

Challenge – We were challenged by what we did over the 500 miles and we challenged ourselves to do it. We had to rise to the unforeseen challenges we met and we did. We can continue to do that rising to the challenge if we let ourselves.

Catholicism – The Way of Saint James is a Roman Catholic pilgrimage route but we were both lapsed Catholics. Could we have walked any other distance route and felt the same about it? Did our former Catholicism make a difference at the time and do we feel any differently about Catholicism after the event? We were raised as cradle Catholics; it was who we were and how we lived and breathed; there was no other option. For our parents this had not been the case. Our father was Jewish and raised as a Jewish boy, converting to Catholicism when he was nineteen years old. Our mother converted to Catholicism when she got married. Our father was a man of science, a medical doctor and loved an intellectual debate, spending many an hour with the parish priest putting the Church to rights. He remained a Catholic until his premature death despite worrying us kids hugely by not attending mass regularly. Our mother, in contrast was very observant as some converts can be. When young our faith was largely a comfort: our guardian angels would look after us; we would go straight to heaven after Saturday confession if we stepped in front of a bus on the way home; heaven was where we all went if we were good and God would answer our prayers if we were sufficiently humble. As we grew to adolescence and adulthood there were inevitable challenging questions that we had, but these were either forbidden to be voiced or were simply not answered. We saw the contradictions between what the Church said and what it did and were revolted by the terrible unkindness of many of the Church's representatives to us and others. We were bowed down by the increasing emphasis on sin and guilt, which was used to get us Catholics to toe the line. All these issues began to make us question our faith. For each of us siblings the final lapsing from the faith was probably caused by different things. For Jane her faith just seemed to drain away – a bit like water down a plug hole; leaving Catholicism was not a conscious or principled stand – the belief had just gone. However, there remained an almost "Pavlovian" reaction when states of emergency or dire need arose – Jane wanted to pray. For Charlotte her faith left her as she sought answers form the nuns in the convent we attended as to how a Good God could, for example, permit the napalming of infants and children in Vietnam. The trite response that we are all given a cross to bear and we must not question God's plan as this was heresy, was totally un-compelling. This together with an emerging political awareness confirmed her atheism. We both continued to want to believe there was at least an energy left when people die and that there was something spiritual in all people. None of these feeling about our lost faith changed on the pilgrimage, except perhaps Jane lost some of the inner feeling of being a hypocritical fraud when dipping back into some of the comforts of faith. At one level we could both appreciate the history of people down the ages treading a pilgrimage path; we did not have to have the reason why explained to us. At another level the spirituality of the Way was also important. We would have permission to privately explore this idea of spirituality on such a path as the other walkers were either people of faith and spirituality or, if they were not, were courteous to those that were. The impact all this had on us, was not to bring us back to any faith, but instead to encourage us to be more accepting of those who are devout – they, for the most part, were not responsible for the sins of omission or commission perpetrated by the bureaucracies that headed their religions – for the evils done in the name of religion. We returned home feeling it was OK to be non-religious, spiritual people. We felt like true pilgrims.

Cathartic – One can get rid of a lot of angst just walking along. The irritations with people's behaviour, with systems and ways of doing things, with many petty things in life – all seem to be gradually left behind as one puts one foot in front of the other. On a less prosaic note, Charlotte found it cathartic to carry out her medal casting ceremonies – sometimes we need a ceremony to appreciate an occasion or a change and these medal ceremonies created a real moment of casting off the anger and upset she associated with the Church.

Clarifying – Many of the "lessons" described in this chapter are not new to us, but the long period of almost six weeks away from home and without work to distract us, allowed us to see some things more clearly. However, on our return home we did not find it easy to summarise what the Camino Way had meant to us. We tended to describe a simple or amusing anecdote about mixed dorms or strange Spanish receptionists; we did not immediately say – "Oh, the Way has made me far less materialistic and more charitable ...." We knew that the walk had affected us, but we needed some time to process our feelings – to clarify our thinking. This book is a sort of culmination of that clarifying process.

Confirmatory – This was one of Jane's final five words in the last blog and its meaning remains a very important outcome from the walk. All the way through the walk Jane had two juxtaposed feelings: homesickness and hopefulness. She missed her husband hugely but was determined to try to complete the pilgrimage. The walk brought home with a vengeance how important her family was to her, far more important than the completion of ambitions such as doing the Camino Way. Charlotte had only just retired from a job that had utterly immersed her – physically and emotionally. She was fearful of being unable to let go of that professional persona that had absorbed her life for so long. However, walking the Way made it not only possible but it was easy. She was able to confirm on her return home that she was a valuable person in her own right.

The Camino Way Pilgrims

Angels:

Angels – We met many a good, kind person on the walk and we in turn tried to be good, kind people. We have described some of these "Camino Angels" to you elsewhere. It is probably easier to be kind when there is a pre-disposition to be that way amongst a majority of the people around you – more challenging when the population is more mixed. We will try to take this kindness lesson forward with us.

The Camino Way Pilgrims

Mourning:

Mourning – Clearly many people walk the Camino Way in remembrance of loved ones who have died. This was not the case for us. However, for Jane there was a sense of loss pervading her life: loss of her children, now grown, who no longer needed her care in the same way as when they were young; loss of herself as a professional woman; loss of youth with all its promise for an exciting future; loss of a self-image as a strong healthy woman. Walking the Way did not resolve all the feelings, but it did help the slow move towards acceptance of herself as a retired woman; one who could still do exciting things and had the strength to do them.

The Camino Way Pilgrims

Intention:

Intention – From the outset we declared our intention to walk the Camino Way. We said it and we then we did it. We have now found that it can help make things happen if we voice our intentions, either to ourselves or to others. For example, Charlotte intended to get rid of many of her possessions on return from Spain and is currently in the process of doing so. She also said she was not going to worry as much, and so far is managing well.

The Camino Way Pilgrims

Nurture:

Nurture – All through the walk we had to look after ourselves and each other. Nurturing was not something we had experienced much of as children, but were surprised to find no problem in nurturing our own children – we could give nurture but often found it difficult to accept it. On the Way we both felt terribly responsible for each other and had to accept help and support many times just to keep going. We were also very appreciative of the support from home, whether through texts, comments on the blog, phone calls and Henry's constant vigilance on our behalf. In addition, given our propensity to work and care for others, actually taking six weeks for ourselves was a risky step into self-nurture that in fact paid off – we have to continue to nurture others, but must not forget our needs as well.

The Camino Way Pilgrims

Openness:

Openness – Charlotte has always been a more gregarious person than Jane, but for both of us we fell happily into the pilgrim propensity to converse with ease and to frequently cut to the chase after the minimum of small talk. This openness was not present everywhere nor with everyone, but was very common. It did allow the development of quick friendships or relationships which gave company, support, courage, amusement and information. Whilst neither of us is likely to become garrulous women nabbing any loiterer on a street corner to chew their ear off, we are trying to make an effort to be a little more open with others and forge those transient connections with another person.

*The Camino **W**ay Pilgrims*

Walking:

Walking – We have already written about the joys and pleasures of walking and how it can be a lovely way to create opportunities for openness with others and to let one's troubles go. Here we see this word as representing our walking through life and the journey ahead of us, on our own but also together with others. Since the Camino Way we still do physically walk and hope to continue – we might even tackle another long distance path of some sort. This clearly requires physical fitness of some degree and in retirement this has to be an objective – to maintain some fitness for that walk through life. Charlotte, in addition, wishes to leave a lighter footprint on the earth and is more thoughtful about how she consumes the world's resources.

*The Camino W **a**y Pilgrims*

Anxiety:

Anxiety – Charlotte had had several years of debilitating anxiety when younger which had profoundly affected her capacity to function. She was very aware of the signs and effects of acute anxiety. This was resolved after a period of counselling. In part, given our unorthodox upbringing, we have a propensity to be anxious and had both been anxious before embarking on the Camino Way. One of our coping strategies had been to obsess about getting the right boots before we set out, finding a place to sleep for the night whilst on the route, worrying about an injury preventing completion of the walk. However, the huge physical effort of walking each day allowed some anxiety to disperse naturally; the adrenalin released by anxiety could not stay pent up, doing damage to the body and mind; the adrenalin was used up naturally through the walking process. All the problems were dealt with successfully. Charlotte is far more aware of how her body responds to anxiety and this awareness has been heightened by the Camino experience. She is now better at recognising what is really causing her anxiety and dealing with it. Jane has to try to put this lesson into practice more.

The Camino Wa**y** Pilgrims

Yearning:

Yearning – We learnt we must do things, live our lives, get on with ambitions – we must not simply yearn after something.

The Camino Way **P**ilgrims

Preparation, People, Prayer, Pilgrimage, Possessions:

Preparation – We succeeded on the Camino Way through perseverance, supporting one another and by being supported, but also by being well-prepared. We had researched the right kit to assemble; we had gone for practice walks to build stamina and trouble-shoot; we had read about what it might be like. Being prepared was not a new idea for either of us, but its usefulness was emphasised to us because many times we were grateful that we had thought something through or brought along the right bit of kit.

People – This was not a solitary walk, so if anyone wants that type of experience, do not do the Camino Frances. There were periods when we hardly met anyone, but on most days there would be other folks either on the Way or in the hostel. These people were of all ages, although at the time of year we went there were probably more older people than younger ones and we saw no children other than two babies being carried by walking parents. We have already written about the pleasures of transient friendships, but here we would like to comment on how much more accepting we became of the idiosyncrasies of the diverse swathe of humanity we came across, whether as pilgrims or the Spanish people living and working where we passed through. There were exceptions, of course – some people puzzled us to the point of exasperation – and there was the one man who was just totally foul. The Camino Way reminded us that one must not judge a book by its cover (unless it is swaying and carrying a bottle!)

Prayer – Jane had been asked to say prayers for various people before she set out on the pilgrimage and, despite not being a person of faith, she did this every day of the walk. There was something very important about sending out good thoughts for those people, wishing them well, that was a bit like praying. It is something that gave Jane a sense of comfort and will probably continue to do so.

Pilgrimage – The Oxford Dictionary defines a pilgrimage as a journey to a sacred place as an act of religious devotion. We have already addressed the issue of religion and that for us this equated to being spiritual. Clearly we were heading to a place deemed by many to be sacred. In our minds, therefore we were pilgrims on a pilgrimage.

Possessions – We carried our possessions on our backs and this came to be a metaphor for what one needs to carry in life. We both felt that on our return from Spain we should endeavour to live our lives with fewer material possessions and be mindful of what we have relative to others.

The Camino Way Pilgrims

International:

International – A huge pleasure along the Way was the wide range of pilgrims of different nationalities from around the world – if we could say nothing in their language, we could say Buen Camino and be understood. Meeting people from Canada and Brazil, Australia and South Africa, Korea and Holland, Germany and Rwanda, Scotland and Zimbabwe, Switzerland and Ireland, United States of America and Italy, France and many other places – made the world seem smaller and that we all have more similarities than differences. Where there is a will to understand each other and to communicate, it can be done.

The Camino Way Pilgrims

Levity, Loneliness:

Levity – We laughed a lot on the journey, at ourselves, at things we saw and did, but we also laughed with many of the pilgrims we met. The simplicity of life on the road encouraged many people to be unburdened from life's concerns and so feel free to enjoy the humour around and in each other's company. We all had a type of almost childlike appreciation of the oddities and silliness in life. We want to try and maintain this light-heartedness in our lives.

Loneliness – Being solitary is not a problem but being lonely is. Although we were walking as two sisters together we both were lonely at times. Having returned from our journey, we both appreciate the need to maintain friendships and to be good friends.

The Camino Way Pilgrims

Guidance:

Guidance – The Camino Way, as we have already indicated, is very well supported. There is a lot of information available about it which helped us prepare. There are physical signs all along the Way to guide the walker. We received advice before we left and from people all along the Way. Much of this was essential to our successful achievement of the journey. The Camino took us down to low points at times, but advice from others allowed us to pick ourselves up again. What we want to take forward is the idea of living our lives recognising that some guidance might be useful as we do not always have all the answers, but also that we might be able to offer guidance to others at times. In the past both of us have not felt comfortable admitting weakness so have not always sought out guidance that would have been helpful.

The Camino Way Pilgrims

Reflection:

Reflection – Charlotte had just retired from working for the National Health Service where she had as a matter of course used reflective practices as a way of working professionally. However, we both anticipated that we would enjoy time to reflect on our retirements and what we wanted to do in the next stages of our lives. We surprised ourselves whilst on the Way that we did precious little reflecting on anything other than the prosaic and the hilarious. On our return from Spain we were again surprised that now we were able to reflect on what it had all meant. This way of thinking and reflecting has become a daily habit for Charlotte.

The Camino Way Pilgrims

Immaterial:

Immaterial – We each must have used the phrase "let it go" any number of times on the journey across Spain. We found gradually that we could let upsets, annoyances, worries go – they were immaterial. Additionally, we had started out with all sorts of labels attached to us such as, "white", "middle-aged", "mother", "grandmother, "not-working", "unwell", "unfit", "middle-class", "married", "single". It was easy to define ourselves in this way and sometimes that was fine. However, labels carry assumptions with them that are not always true or helpful. On the Way, such labels diminished in importance; we were just pilgrims and made few assumptions about others we met. We are both now less needful of defining labels. Our society places much importance on status-giving labels. We now feel freer to create our own labels – we are strong women who completed the Camino Way.

*The Camino Way Pilgrim*s

Miracles:

Miracles- Wonders do happen.

*The Camino Way Pilgrim***s**

Self-esteem, Sisters:

Self-esteem – For both of us as we set off our self-esteem was not at its highest. Broadly speaking we were strong, confident and independent women. Chronic health conditions and issues around recent retirements had knocked that confidence. Completing the Camino Frances has re-established our self-esteem. Such an achievement is life-affirming, life-enhancing and life-enriching. It would be difficult to return with one's sense of self unchanged.

Sisters – We met many configurations of people travelling together. There were numerous husbands and wives and couples of both genders, groups of friends, a few mothers and daughters and at least one mother and son. There were many solo walkers. There were also charitable groups and some church groups. But we met no other sisters walking together. Both before we left on the journey and on our return, many people commented on how extraordinary it was that we were walking together for such a length of time. They said that in their cases they would probably kill their sibling, or fall out massively or give up after a couple days. Only one person said that they would love to do such a walk with their sibling. Well, we did not kill each other, nor did we fall out massively. We did learn patience, tolerance and understanding of each other's differences. It confirmed that we loved each other and always had done. The family love that was forged in our strange childhood survived the inevitable sibling battles and has developed into a long-lasting loving loyalty. The Camino Way simply confirmed all this as we had the luxury of time in such an unusual context to engage with each other. We would hope some of this family love and loyalty will be our legacy to our children and grandchildren.

So that is us, the two Piney sisters and this was an account of the Way of the Piney Sisters. We had an extraordinary experience travelling across Spain. For us it was more than just a six week holiday from home – it was a journey, a pilgrimage. We came back changed from our experience, even though we were not entirely aware of those changes for some time. Most of those alterations would not be obvious to others, but should make a difference to the way we lead our lives. It was exhausting yet it was enormous fun. Sometimes we cannot believe we did it. This book will create tangible proof to us that we did. So as a farewell, Dear Reader and a thank you for staying with us to this point we say to you:

Buen Camino!

ABOUT THE AUTHORS

Jane Ball lives in East Sussex with her husband, Henry. Charlotte Piney lives in Sheffield, South Yorkshire. This is their first book. They walked the Camino Frances from 2nd May to 10th June 2013.

4425311R00159

Printed in Germany
by Amazon Distribution
GmbH, Leipzig